BILLIE HOLIDAY

THE
TRAGEDY AND TRIUMPH
OF
LADY DAY

LESLIE
GOURSE

An Impact Biography

Franklin Watts
A Division of Grolier Publishing
New York/London/Hong Kong/Sydney
Danbury, Connecticut

The author gratefully acknowledges the following for use of copyrighted material:
Excerpts from *From Satchmo to Miles*, by Leonard Feather, published by
Stein and Day and Da Capo Press, used with permission of the author.
From Billie Holiday, by Bud Kliment, Chelsea House Publishers,
(1990, by Chelsea House Publishers, a division of Main Line Book Co.,
New York and Philadelphia).
From Lady Sings the Blues by Billie Holiday and William F. Dufty. Copyright 1956
by Eleanora Fagan and William F. Dufty. Used by permission of Doubleday,
a division of Bantam Doubleday Dell Publishing Group, Inc.
Excerpts from *Lady Day: The Many Faces of Billie Holiday*, by
Robert O'Meally, used with permission of Little, Brown and Company.
Excerpt reprinted from *Variety*, (1948, by Cahners Publishing Company).
"God Bless the Child," Billie Holiday, Arthur Herzog, Jr. Copyright 1941 Edward B.
Marks Music Company. Copyright Renewed. Used by permission. All rights reserved.

Photographs copyright ©: Frank Driggs Collection: pp. 9, 12, 18, 38, 42, 47, 51,
55, 67, 69, 72, 74, 78, 88, 93, 109, 116; UPI/Bettman: pp.24, 105, 113;
Bettmann Archive: p.34; NYPL Picture Collection: pp. 58, 82, 97, 111 (Jean Pierre
LeCoir); AP/Wide World Photos: pp. 89, 103.

Library of Congress Cataloging-in-Publication Data

Gourse, Leslie.
    Billie Holiday: the tragedy and triumph of Lady Day / by Leslie Gourse.
        p. cm.—(An Impact biography)
    Includes bibliographical references, index, and discography.
    Summary: Relates the story of an Afro–American woman who, despite a turbulent life,
        became one of the most famous singers in the history of jazz.
    ISBN 0-531-11248-9 (lib. bdg.). – ISBN 0-531-15753-9 (pbk.)
    1. Holiday, Billie, 1915–1959—Juvenile literature. 2. Women jazz musicians—
            United States—Biography—Juvenile literature.
        3. Singers—United States—Biography—Juvenile literature.
    [1. Holiday, Billie, 1915–1959. 2. Singers. 3. Afro-Americans—Biography.
                4. Women—Biography.]
                    I. Title. II. Series.
            ML3930.H64G68   1995
            782.42165'092—dc20
[B]   94-17462
                                                                  CIP
                                                                 AC M

CONTENTS

BILLIE HOLIDAY

BILLIE HOLIDAY PERSONIFIES
THE SOUND OF JAZZ

In December 1957, the Columbia Broadcasting System (CBS) presented a television show about jazz. It was part of a series called *The Seven Lively Arts*. Jazz was then slowly coming to be recognized as one of the great American arts. Many of the early jazz players and singers had suffered through hardships and insults because they performed emotionally stirring music that had gotten its start on the wrong side of the tracks. Musicians often played in nightclubs, after-hours clubs, gambling houses, brothels, and speakeasies that sold illegal, bootleg whiskey in African-American neighborhoods during Prohibition. Jazz was also played in white neighborhoods such as the white section of Storyville in New Orleans, where whites had the same sort of entertainment and houses for partying. But the African-American jazz musicians, who had invented the syncopated rhythms and embellished melodies of jazz, suffered most of all.

They were persecuted by segregation—the official separation of the races in most public places. Racial prejudice dogged their steps as they toured the United States, playing in small groups and big bands, unable to eat, sleep, or wash in the same restaurants, hotels, and facilities with whites. The prejudice against African-Americans carried over to their new free-spirited music. It was not accorded the respect it should have gotten.

The civil rights movement to correct the injustices against African-Americans and improve their lives was just beginning to take effect when CBS presented *The Seven Lively Arts*, a television series that presented the best in American arts and culture. It would be another decade before jazz would begin to be taught in schools in 1968. Not until then would the National Endowment for the Arts start awarding financial grants to jazz artists—both African-American innovators and white contributors—for study and performances.

But many white people had loved and respected jazz since its earliest days. They became fans and champions of the jazz players and helped them achieve recognition as great creative artists. Some people at CBS knew how important jazz was. So CBS decided to include jazz, performed by great players, as part of the arts and culture series in 1957.

One of the most famous African-Americans in the jazz world was singer Billie Holiday. She was a tall, statuesque woman with a distinctive voice and style. No one ever mistook her sweet, dreamy sound for anyone else's. She made sudden octave jumps and landed true on high notes that other singers would have missed by a mile and sung out of tune. She had a lazy way of improvising melodies—changing and embellishing the tunes and giving them a bluesy, melancholy feeling. She accented her ideas with unusual pauses, rhythmic emphases, and even pretty musical whines to express a song's lyrics. And she punctuated her songs with surprising staccato chirps. No other singer did that.

It almost didn't matter what words she was singing. The soft, plaintive quality of her voice really told her stories. Sometimes she sounded as if she was laughing when she sang. And especially when her voice became raspy from the wear and tear of her life's experiences, she could sound as if her heart was breaking from disappointment. All her life, one of her most important techniques was to listen carefully to the instru-

Billie Holiday

ments playing with her. Then she blended with them or wended her way around their lines with catlike grace.

In 1956, Billie had signed a contract to record for CBS. So she was a natural choice to sing with a group of prominent male instrumentalists asked to play for the TV special. One of the men performing with her was her old friend, tenor saxophonist Lester Young. They had met about twenty years earlier and had played together in a famous blues-based big band led by Count Basie. That band toured the country in Basie's bus, called the Blue Goose, weathered the insults of racial prejudice, and won the love of audiences. Long before 1957, the band had become world famous.

Billie and Lester had always performed together with exceptional beauty and sweet communion. Music poured from them as slowly as honey could drip. Lester had the smoothest, most mellow sound of all the saxophonists, and often Billie sounded exactly like him. Both had small, quiet sounds. Neither of them ever belted or screeched a song. Very close friends, but never sweethearts, even before they had toured with Basie, they had gone to clubs in Harlem and listened to music together. And for the love of music, without pay, they had performed in jam sessions.

Eventually they drifted apart. Nobody knew exactly what quarrel or difference of opinion separated them for a while. But they lost touch with each other. For most of their adult lives, both suffered from deep-seated personal problems. Lester became an alcoholic. Billie started taking heroin. Then she too became an alcoholic. When they were reunited for the taping of the CBS show, the music they made together radiated their affection for each other and their musical kinship.

For the show, which was taped in black-and-white, all the musicians dressed in casual clothes. Lester wore his trademark porkpie hat. Billie pulled her lustrous hair straight back from her temples. The style called attention to the fine bones and shape of her oval face. She had a pretty little nose and an exquisite, regal-looking profile. As usual by that time, she brought a bottle of gin and cans of Coca-Cola to the studio. She drank and smoked continuously when she wasn't singing. The audience didn't see that. Strangers rarely had a view of anything but her charm during a performance.

She sang a blues number called "Fine and Mellow," which she had first recorded with her own orchestra in 1939, four years after she began her recording career. Certain songs would always be associated with Billie. That was one of them. She and Lester performed it for CBS with their languid, plaintive sounds. With her eyes shining, she watched him raptly, joyfully, while he played. A slight smile curved her lips. Her head swayed slowly to signify that she was mesmerized by his smooth, fluid style.

Emulating him, she sang the lyrics lazily: "Love is just like a faucet,/ It turns off and on,/ Love is just like a faucet,/ It turns off and on./ Sometimes when you think it's on, baby,/ It has turned off and gone."

That was a story that Billie knew about in her personal life very well. But when she was singing, she could rise above the sad message and feel happy. Her dreamy expression may have been caused, too, by the alcohol she had been drinking. The previous year she had stopped taking heroin, and she had soon substituted alcohol to steady her nerves. The audience for this television special had no idea of her personal troubles, because her performance was so romantic and seductive.

Still photographs of Billie were taken from the show for use on the covers of her record albums. Those photos quickly became a symbol of jazz. They are used even to this day for books, albums, advertisements, posters, T-shirts, and every type of jazz-related enterprise. Billie's face alone has become an icon, a symbol, of jazz.

She looked so radiantly beautiful on that show that most of the audience didn't worry that the slender woman, who seemed to be entranced, with her moist, luminous eyes and a mysterious half-smile, no longer presented herself as a plump, alert, and healthy-looking girl with a broad smile. That was how she had looked at the start of her career. "The sight of this tall, buxom, beautiful girl with exquisite coloring was enough to

Billie Holiday in 1957: her emotional singing and mysterious beauty had made her a symbol of jazz and the blues.

make any neck swivel," wrote John Chilton, the author of *Billie's Blues*, a biography of the singer, about her appearance on the Apollo Theatre's stage early in her career, when she was a teenager. "On looks alone, Billie was potential star material, but her voice was her greatest asset, for she sang in a style that was new to the world."

For the CBS show, her voice was no longer clear and fresh. But her star quality, her singing style, and her passion for music had endured. What she had lost in animation, she replaced with feeling. Despite all her problems behind the scenes, the video she helped make that day became known as *The Sound of Jazz*, one of the most famous films in jazz history. It was an easily understood testimony to the hypnotic power of jazz and the artistry of the pioneering musicians.

She died a year and a half later. When her friends in the jazz world got the news, they played her recording of "Gloomy Sunday," another of her famous songs. By then the newspapers had publicized how ill she had become from the substances she used to steady her nerves. But through the strength of her unshakable devotion to music and her charisma, she had established herself, with her eccentric sound, as a great singer for her time and for all time.

Before she was a teenager, she had been beaten, abused, abandoned, and even jailed in a reformatory. Her mother wasn't around all the time to raise her. Her father, a traveling musician, was never around, except for brief visits. An aunt who helped to raise her was especially cruel. Then Billie learned to live on her own, using her wits and her singing talent to earn money and get some fun out of life. When she sang, people respected her. But Billie grew up to become easily entranced and influenced by people who lived thrill-seeking, dangerous lives in the fast lane, and people who had little time or inclination to care about her welfare. Those self-absorbed people were the type Billie had always known best. Love and acceptance never came easily to her.

When she was building a career in her teens and twenties, club owners sometimes made fun of her quiet, slow style of singing. They wanted flashy, upbeat singers to rock the house. As an African-American, too, Billie was constantly running into prejudice and barriers. Called names and shoved aside, she became a drug addict when she was twenty-five years old. After that, newspapers often put her name in the headlines for reasons other than her remarkable singing voice and artistic, unique style. She was arrested, forced to go to trial several times, and jailed for nearly a year. The public became familiar and fascinated with tales of her wild lifestyle. No singer was written about so much in newspapers and magazines, usually for the wrong reasons.

Her albums would always have liner notes filled with information—and misinformation—about her life. She wrote a book about herself, called *Lady Sings the Blues*. Her best friends knew that she invented some of the story. She blended fact and fiction so that she could hide the saddest facts. She didn't really want to discuss them. When Billie started singing the blues song popularized by Bessie Smith, "Ain't Nobody's Business if I Do," she really meant that it was nobody's business what she had done or would do to survive. She simply needed the money from the book, and so she decided to produce an entertaining story to sell to a public that was eager to hear about her hard times and successes. She was completely truthful only on stage and in recordings. Lester Young had given her the nickname and title "Lady" when she was starting her career. In return she called him "President of the Tenor Saxophone." Soon everyone was calling him Prez, and Billie became Lady Day. She wanted to live up to the title, and as a singer she did.

Her haunting, sometimes even eerie sound had a mysterious effect on audiences. It made them feel happy, because they could identify with feelings she expressed about her troubled life. Her artistry also helped audiences overcome their sadnesses and disappointments. People relaxed and sat totally still when Lady, as her friends called her, sang to them about the truth. In her small, pretty voice, capable of creating new, blue-sounding melodies, they heard the sound of nostalgia—a longing for missed opportunities and lost love. When Billie bared her soul, she did it with whimsy that allowed her to transcend her troubles. When she was singing, she was truly the Lady.

Fifteen years after she died, a movie was made about her life. Her old fans went to see it. The film brought her new fans, too. They didn't know or care that the story was even more fanciful than Billie's inventions in her own book. There are few reliable sources about Billie's early life. So even with all the recordings, the books, and the film about Billie, she has remained mysterious. In recent years, jazz historians have tried to dig deeper for the facts. Musicians and others who knew Billie have helped by contributing information. A portrait has emerged of a woman who never had loving or stable guidance as a child. Nobody helped her make wise decisions and take care of her mind and body. But she had an instinctive musical genius. She knew exactly what she was doing when she stood in front of a microphone. Through her songs she has achieved immortality and a state of grace. "Lady Day" is a title that commands respect.

ELEANORA
BECOMES BILLIE

Sadie Fagan was working as a maid in Philadelphia when she gave birth to her only child, Eleanora, on April 7, 1915, and had her baptized a Catholic in the hospital. (It would be at least another dozen years before Eleanora Fagan began to call herself Billie Holiday.) Sadie wasn't married to Eleanora's father, Clarence Holiday, a budding jazz guitarist whom Sadie had met at a festival in Baltimore, their hometown.

Eleanora's mother was actually a nice, hardworking young woman who had fallen in love, gotten pregnant, and found out that her boyfriend was no longer in love with her. He certainly didn't want to get married. So Sadie had left Baltimore and gone to Philadelphia to have her child. Her Baltimore neighborhood was full of gossips, and her quiet, respectable family was embarrassed by Sadie. Her father, Charles Fagan, had worked all his life as a chef. According to a prizewinning book about Billie Holiday, Sadie Fagan herself had been born out of wedlock to Charles Fagan and a woman whose last name was Harris. Later he married another woman. Sadie felt close to her father and may have lived with him when she was a teenager. But his wife never particularly liked having a stepdaughter around. Sadie's pregnancy out of wedlock made her relations with her stepmother even more awkward.

When Eleanora was born, Sadie Fagan was nineteen and Clarence Holiday was seventeen. He admitted that Eleanora was his child, and he thought the light-skinned baby was pretty. But he didn't want to help Sadie raise and protect their daughter. He had set his heart on becoming a professional musician and traveling on the road with a big, swinging jazz band. When he found out that he had to learn to read music to get a job, he studied hard for a year.

He also liked to dress in sharp-looking clothes and socialize with people who hustled for their livelihood. His friends were people who went out at night—struggling musicians who played wherever they could find a gig, and he even managed to feel at home among the gamblers, prostitutes, pimps, and other hustlers who were a part of the nightlife. He had such a fast way of talking that his friends nicknamed him Lib Lab. That was the jazz musicians' witty way of saying "ad lib," a term describing a musician's own creative phrases with which he decorated a song.

One day Billie Holiday would write a book that depicted her family situation the way she wished it had been. She wrote: "Mom and Pop were just a couple of kids when they got married. He was eighteen, she was sixteen, and I was three." But her parents never got married.

Eleanora was already old enough to sit up in a carriage when her mother took her home to their relatives in Baltimore. Some of them didn't want anything to do with Sadie because she had given birth to a child out of wedlock. She and Eleanora went to live with Sadie's brother for a while in West Baltimore, a neighborhood that Eleanora would think of as "fancy." Then Sadie rented places of her own in poorer neighborhoods. And she had to move often because she was always short of money. She earned very little from her jobs as a maid and a cook.

When Eleanora was five, Sadie met a longshoreman named Phil Gough, who married her. Grandfather Charles Fagan helped them buy a house in West Baltimore. Sadie's mar-

Little Eleanora at age three: the future Billie Holiday endured a difficult childhood in which she and her mother moved to new homes many times.

riage made her acceptable to her relatives. Eleanora was very happy and prayed that the good times would last. But after a few years Sadie and Phil Gough separated. Sadie was unable to make payments alone on the house, and she had to give it up. Her family looked down on her again.

Realizing that she could never earn as much money as a maid in Baltimore as she could in the North, Sadie decided to leave Eleanora with the family in Baltimore and go back to Philadelphia. She would save money, return to claim her daughter, and make a better life for them together. Eleanora went to live with Sadie's brother, John, and his wife, Ida. Eleanora would soon realize that Ida was very mean. They lived in a crowded house with Eleanora's maternal grandparents, Charles Fagan and his wife, and Eleanora's maternal great-grandmother. Aunt Ida had always picked on Sadie for being a single mother. When she went north, Ida made fun of Eleanora for having no father in the house. Ida always threatened her by saying that she would grow up "bad" the way her mother did.

Eleanora, who was about eight years old, already liked to sing. She may have learned blues and popular love songs from the radio. The songs, which were always referring to "my man," aggravated her Aunt Ida, who thought they were sinful, especially for a child to sing. But Eleanora kept singing them. Not only the radio, but her father, when he visited, may have taught her some tunes. He had a pleasant voice with a lazy style, and he was known as a good rhythm player on his guitar. It was his job to strum the rhythm in the bands that hired him. Sometimes he sang with the bands, too.

Eleanora, who grew tall and strong quickly, tried to be a helpful girl. She remembered being very young when she first went out with a pail, soap, and brushes to scrub the white stone steps of the houses in Baltimore. She earned fifteen cents for each set of steps. Sometimes she had to wash a bathroom or kitchen floor for that money, too.

Ida had two young children of her own, Henry and Elsie. Eleanora and her cousins slept in the same bed. That was no fun for the girls. Henry used to wet the bed and hit them. They didn't get much sleep because they had to fight him off all night. In the morning they were so tired that they went to school late. When Aunt Ida found the bed wet, she blamed Eleanora and beat her with her fists or sometimes even with a whip. Aunt Ida didn't want to believe that her dear little Henry had wet the bed.

Though Henry grew up to be a minister, as a boy he was a rascal. One time he swung a dead rat by its tail in front of Eleanora's face in the street. She begged him to stop, but he wouldn't, and so she hit him hard. She recalled that the family had to take him to a hospital to get care for his bruises. Even while she was still in grammar school, she was learning to fight and protect herself. She also liked to play baseball and roller-skate with the boys on the baseball team. Her father nicknamed her "Bill" for her tomboyish ways. That name appealed to her much more than 'Nora. Her Aunt Ida always called her 'Nora when she yelled for her to do something.

Eleanora's stepgrandmother—Sadie's stepmother—had little interest in her. Eleanora thought her grandfather was happy to have her around. But her best friend in the family was her great-grandmother, whom Eleanora called Grandma. "She really loved me, and I was crazy about her," Eleanora would write in her autobiography. Eleanora was her grandma's only real friend, too. Nobody else bothered with them.

Grandma was about ninety-five years old. Her legs were always sore and needed to be wrapped in clean bandages daily. When Eleanora left school, she washed steps. Then she went home to bathe Grandma and change and wash the leg bandages. Eleanora sat with Grandma for hours while the old woman told her stories about slavery days on the white-owned plantations in the South. Grandma told Eleanora what it had felt like to be owned body and soul by a white man. She had borne sixteen children to that man. Grandma couldn't read, but she could recite stories from the Bible to Eleanora. The child loved to hear Grandma talk.

Among her other ills, Grandma had edema, which everyone called by its commonly used name, dropsy. It meant that life-threatening fluid gathered in parts of her body. If she lay down, it could gather in her stomach and probably her lungs, too, and kill her. Grandma always slept sitting up in a chair. But one day she felt so tired that she begged Eleanora to help her lie down on the floor. Eleanora didn't want to help her get out of the chair, because she had never seen Grandma take a nap lying down. But the old woman pleaded. Eleanora spread a blanket on the floor. Together they lay down. Grandma started telling her a story. But Eleanora was tired from school and scrubbing, and she fell asleep quickly.

When she woke up a few hours later, she noticed that Grandma wasn't breathing. Grandma had died. And she had one arm around Eleanora. The arm had grown stiff. Eleanora couldn't get loose from Grandma's embrace. She screamed until the neighbors came running. They broke one of Grandma's arms, in which rigor mortis had set in, and freed the child. She was so shocked and heartbroken that she had to go to a hospital to recover. When she came home after a month, her Aunt Ida started beating her as usual. This time it was for having let Grandma get out of her chair. A doctor saw Ida beating Eleanora. "He said if she kept it up, I'd grow up to be nervous. But she never stopped," Eleanora wrote in her autobiography.

She was rescued from Aunt Ida by her mother, who came back to Baltimore with nine hundred dollars and took Eleanora to live in an apartment. Sadie planned to take in boarders. She also soon found a boyfriend, a porter, whose last name was Hill. Called Wee Wee as a nickname by everyone, he had a steady job in a building in downtown Baltimore. Wee Wee loved Sadie, even though she was eight years older than he. Sadie was a pretty little woman, about five feet tall, and very light-skinned, like Eleanora. Eleanora was always asking her pretty mother to dress up in a bright red hat, which Sadie had made for herself. Eleanora thought it looked like the glamorous hats that the well-dressed prostitutes in the neighborhood wore. Even though she was a child, about ten years old, Eleanora was very alert to the people and their activities in the streets around her. She wasn't slick yet. Actually she was innocent and didn't have any interest in sex. But she noticed the pretty things money could buy, and she was coming to know about the kinds of jobs, legal and illegal, that people could choose to do.

One day, when she came home from school, she discovered her mother was out. A man who lived in the neighborhood came into the house and told her that Sadie had asked him to take Eleanora to another neighbor's house. Sadie would pick her daughter up there. The man, whom Eleanora knew as Mr. Dick, took her by the hand and led her to a brothel. She was maturing fast physically, developing a curvy body that made her look far older than her age. Mr. Dick guided her into a bedroom and tried to force her to have sexual relations with him. She screamed and fought him. At the same time, Sadie was being tipped off by a prostitute who knew Mr. Dick. Sadie ran into the brothel with some policemen. Even though Eleanora was bleeding from her fight with Mr. Dick, the police arrested her, too.

The next day Mr. Dick was sentenced to five years in jail for attacking her. Sadie pleaded that she wanted to take Eleanora home. But a judge in juvenile court decided the child was "a minor without proper care and guardianship" and ordered her to spend time in a Catholic institution, the House of the Good Shepherd for Colored Girls. It was a type of reform school, and it was strict.

Many years later, a teacher who worked there recalled Eleanora as a very quiet, shy girl. She sat alone all the time. It made her very happy when the teacher took an interest in her and gave her a prayer book. Eleanora asked to be baptized again in the institution. The teacher thought that she was a good girl, no trouble at all.

But somehow Eleanora broke a rule and was forced to wear an old red dress that girls wore when they were punished. When a girl had that dress on, the other girls were not supposed to talk to her. Eleanora was punished at Easter time. Her mother brought her a basket filled with two fried chicken, hard-boiled eggs, and other good food for the holiday. "Because I had the red dress on, the sisters gave my basket to the other girls and made me sit there and watch them eat it," Eleanora wrote in her autobiography. The sisters also locked her up in a room for a night with the body of a girl who had died at the school. Eleanora banged on the door and screamed all night. The next time she saw her mother, she told her that "if she ever wanted to see me again, she better get me out of there," she wrote in her book. Sadie enlisted the help of some wealthy white people for whom she was working as a maid. They went to a judge, who freed Eleanora to go home with her mother.

The girl went back to work, washing steps, trying hard to help her mother make ends meet. Wee Wee Hill and Sadie were living together. Sadie finally got a divorce from Phil Gough, who had been gone for a long time, and Sadie thought she would like to marry Hill. But he ran around with young girlfriends. He wasn't willing to settle down and live a quiet, stable life. So he and Sadie had some bad fights. Eleanora saw her mother hit Wee Wee.

It may seem that Eleanora never had any joy in life, but that isn't so. She was always happy when she lived with her mother. And she discovered the new popular jazz and blues recordings. As she was washing the steps, she came to a brothel owned by a woman named Alice Dean. The house was on a corner near the house where Eleanora lived. She always charged a nickel or a dime for running errands to the stores for everyone else, but she did everything free for Alice and the girls who worked for her. "When it came time to pay me, I used to tell her she could keep the money if she'd let me come up in her front parlor and listen to Louis Armstrong and Bessie Smith on her Victrola."

A Victrola was a prized possession in those days. Eleanora spent wonderful hours listening to the records. In 1928, trumpeter and singer Louis Armstrong had made a classic recording of "West End Blues," on which he hummed and scatted a tune. It had the dreamy beauty of a reverie. Eleanora was thirteen years old that year. "It was the first time I heard anybody sing without using any words," she recalled about Armstrong's style. "I didn't know he was singing whatever came

In her teens, Eleanora loved listening to Louis Armstrong records. Armstrong was famous for his trumpet playing first, and audiences loved his occasional singing so much that he sang more and more often. His distinctive, improvisational "scatting" style influenced young Eleanora as a singer.

into his head when he forgot the lyrics. Ba ba ba ba ba ba ba and the rest of it had plenty of meaning for me—just as much meaning as some of the other words that I didn't always understand. But the meaning used to change, depending on how I felt. Sometimes the record would make me so sad I'd cry up a storm. Other times the same damn record would make me so happy I'd forget about how much hard-earned money the session in the parlor was costing me."

Eleanora didn't care that she had been introduced to the enchanting music in a brothel. If she had heard it coming from a minister's window, she would have climbed into his house to hear it. But it would be many years before ministers, priests, and eventually rabbis began to take an interest in jazz. Singer Bessie Smith's powerful voice lifted Eleanora's spirits and horizons, too. She liked to sing along note for note with Bessie's recordings, and she wished that she had a big, loud voice like Bessie's. Using her soft, pretty little voice, Eleanora imitated Armstrong's relaxed phrasing and rhythms.

Her father's example encouraged her to love music, too. She knew that a big band hired him that year, 1928, and he went on the road to tour the country. He was a distant but romantic figure for her to wonder about. It pleased her to share his love for music.

She was also fond of other good things in life—white silk stockings and black patent leather shoes, for example. She did not have money to buy them, so she shoplifted the stockings from a five-and-dime store counter. She also liked to eat hot dogs. She wasn't supposed to be served at the store's segregated lunch counter, because she was "colored," as people called African-Americans in those days. But the clerks sold her hot dogs anyway. To protect their jobs, they made her promise not to eat the hot dogs in plain sight. She had to wait until she got out on the street. That was all right with Eleanora. She was getting her way.

She also loved to go to the movies, but she didn't want to spend her hard-earned food money. So she found a way to sneak in a back door of the movie theater, she later claimed in her autobiography. She also sometimes paid a nickel or a dime for a ticket and went with friends. Sitting in the dark theater, with her heart beating fast, she watched a lovely young actress named Billie Dove play romantic roles in Hollywood films. Eleanora saw every film that Billie Dove ever made. The movies inspired Eleanora to dream of escaping from the poverty and dreariness of her life in Baltimore, where she and her mother were regarded as the black sheep of their family. Eleanora noticed, however, that none of her relatives, despite all their hard work, could get ahead, either. Wages were low. Living conditions were difficult. She admired her father's lifestyle much more. She didn't want to grow up to be a maid, without hope of improving her lot. She wanted to become an actress, a dancer—something that would lift her life.

First she arranged her hair the way Billie Dove did hers. Then Eleanora started calling herself Billie. It was a perfect name, a feminine version of her father's nickname for her. She began introducing herself to people as Billie.

Around that time, her father married a West Indian woman named Fanny, who lived in Philadelphia. When he came to Baltimore, he visited Billie and noticed that she was growing physically big and tall. She was street smart, too—able to take care of herself in the streets as well as a boy could. If someone tried to push her around, she fought back. She did not seem to be afraid of anybody.

Sadie decided to go north again to work as a maid. Her plan was to go with Wee Wee Hill and send for her daughter soon. Billie boarded with a family, probably Wee Wee's mother; she took in tenants. Billie was supposed to be going to school, but nobody forced her to go anymore. Her mother, herself so inconsistent and uncertain of her plans that she had never been able to give Billie a dependable routine or proper guidance and protection, was gone again. Billie played hooky. She later said that she never got beyond the fifth grade.

Music continued to delight her. She began to be drawn to Baltimore's nightlife and the places where she could hear music and sing. At night she dressed up and went to the brothels, clubs, apartments, and houses where people danced, sang, and played their own instruments to please themselves and each other. Billie met musicians and learned about music from them. She sang all the time, with and without accompaniment, and she discovered that people liked to hear her sing. They gave her tips. Her voice remained small, but it was full of life, light, and high.

A few of her friends, who were denizens of the nightlife, later told researchers looking for information about Billie's early life that they never saw her wash steps. Instead, they said, they had seen her working as a singer in brothels. She was pretty and young, and other women were jealous of her because her singing charmed the men. Some people said they saw her wearing little satin gowns in brothels. They thought she worked as a prostitute, too. When the party was over in such a house, she headed for nightclubs with her friends. They went club-hopping until two or three in the morning. She was always singing everyplace in Baltimore. Then she went to the after-hours clubs—places where people smoked cigarettes and marijuana, drank gin, and entertained one another with music. She also sang at rent parties where musicians were hired to play. Guests paid to listen, eat soul food, and drink liquor. The money they paid went for an apartment's rent.

Several jazz historians have worked hard to find out the exact facts about Billie's childhood. They have different ideas about where Billie lived in Baltimore and why she was sent to live in a Catholic school. People who knew her didn't keep good track of the details, because they hadn't realized she would grow up to be so famous and interesting.

A few things are certain about Billie's nighttime activities. When she left her boardinghouse at night wearing high-heeled shoes and makeup, she looked much older than she was. So she could go wherever she pleased. Some people say she stood about six feet tall when she grew to her full height by her midteens. Others say she was much shorter than that, but so striking, big, and powerful that she looked taller than she actually was. Listening to records and other musicians, she developed a good ear for jazz. She learned to treat her voice as another instrument, especially a horn, in a group, and she could perform many of the tricks that the horn players did. From watching more mature singers and musicians, she began to learn stagecraft, keeping very still, holding her hands steady, with one hand up a little, the other at her side. And she just let the songs flow out of her.

Her mother may have heard that Billie was running wild. Sadie, who was working for a woman in a suburb of New York City, sent word that it was time for her to go north. Planning to join her mother, Billie got on a train. But a powerful urge to see Harlem was driving her. Harlem had developed into a lively community of African-American artists—musicians, singers, dancers, comedians, writers, actors, painters, songwriters, and social thinkers, too—in the 1920s. From musicians in Baltimore, Billie had heard about the Cotton Club, a glamorous place where very talented African-Americans performed. Every musician with any ambition and love for music and entertainment wanted to try his or her luck in Harlem. Billie's father played in Harlem and downtown sometimes with a band, she knew. She also knew that when she joined her mother, Sadie would find a job for her as a maid. Billie hated the thought. By the time she got off the train in New York City, with nothing but a little suitcase and a small basket of food someone had given her for the trip, she had decided that somehow she was going to wind up in Harlem, hear the music, and join in the fun.

The year was 1930; Billie was fifteen years old.

HOME
TO HARLEM

Billie was right. Sadie, who was working in a suburb, found her a job as a maid nearby. Billie suffered with the job for a while. When she refused to wash a rug, she was fired. Good riddance, she thought.

So Sadie took her to a Harlem boardinghouse run by a woman whom Sadie thought was a successful businesswoman with a gambling parlor. Billie was supposed to earn her keep by cleaning the rooms and running errands. But the boardinghouse was really a brothel. Soon Billie, a very pretty, healthy-looking, light-skinned youngster, was working as a prostitute herself. She earned more money in a week than she could have dreamed of earning in a long stretch of time as a maid, and that pleased her. She hadn't been working as a prostitute for very long when one of the customers—a gangster who wielded some influence with the police—had her arrested because she refused to have sexual relations with him. He was big and brutal-looking. She was afraid of him.

Her mother came running to help her. Sadie had to swear that Billie was eighteen years old. If the police had found out she was only fifteen, they would have sent her to reform school for years. She went to jail for several months, then headed back to Harlem. Needing money, she again worked as a prostitute briefly.

Billie eventually took a job as a waitress at a club in Jamaica, Queens, and sang occasionally in other clubs in Queens and in Brooklyn. A saxophone and clarinet player, Kenneth Hollon, who later recorded with Billie, worked with her, earning tips, in little clubs from 1930 to 1932.

Then Sadie Fagan, who had ended her relationship with Wee Wee Hill, became sick and no longer able to work. She and Billie shared several apartments in New York City in the early 1930s. They were living on 139th Street and Seventh Avenue, in the heart of Harlem, by 1932. And they were always in need of money. Sadie had begun to think wishfully about Clarence Holiday and was using his last name. Billie was calling herself Billie Halliday, a variation on the charming family name, when she sang for tips.

To help out with money for her herself and her sick mother, Billie went downtown in Manhattan to a dance hall where her father was working with Fletcher Henderson's big band. Billie called out to him backstage, "Daddy!" Clarence was embarrassed because Billie was so big. He wanted to impress the young girls who gathered around him. Musicians in the limelight always attracted female fans. Billie made him seem like a middle-aged man. Clarence told her, "Don't call me Daddy in front of all these people." Billie replied: "I'm going to call you Daddy all night unless you give me some money." He gave Billie money to get rid of her.

One night Billie went home to find that Sadie had become so sick with a stomach ailment that she couldn't even get out of bed. "For the first time since I could remember, Mom was too sick to make it to Mass on Sunday," Billie later recalled. Not only did they have no money for food, but the landlord was threatening to evict them in the morning, in the middle of a very cold winter. Billie knew she had to do something fast. She headed out into the street.

She had the bright idea to go to a nightclub and try her luck at dancing. She was under the impression that dancers, who shook their bodies a little, could earn more money than singers. The first place she thought about was the Cotton Club, which was famous for its excellent chorus line of light-skinned dancers. As she mulled over the possibilities, she walked down Seventh Avenue to 133rd Street, where there were many well-known music clubs, cafés, restaurants, and after-hours places. One of them was called Pod's and Jerry's. The lights were bright and inviting. She opened the door, looked in, and saw a piano player. The customers might be persuaded to give her tips, she thought.

She went to the bar and ordered a glass of gin. She was used to drinking. With a glass in her hand, she could pass herself off as an adult, she had learned. She told the boss that she wanted to try out for a job as a dancer. He told her to go ahead and audition. Unfortunately she knew only a few steps and kept repeating them. "It was pitiful," she later recalled. The boss told her to stop wasting his time and get out. She kept begging for the job. Then the piano player took pity on her and said, "Girl, can you sing?"

Billie was surprised. "I had been singing all my life, but I enjoyed it too much to think I could make any real money at it," she later reminisced. She was still that naive about her talent. But she needed forty-five dollars by morning. She told the piano player, "Sure, I can sing." She asked him to play a song called "Trav'lin' All Alone." "That came closer than anything to the way I felt," she recalled. After she finished singing, people stared at her with tears in their eyes. She picked up thirty-eight dollars in tips from the floor, then sang all night to earn a total of one hundred and fourteen dollars. She gave half of her tips to the piano player. That was the custom in Harlem clubs in those days.

The pianist was Bobby Henderson, who became Billie's regular accompanist at Pod's and Jerry's. In her autobiography, she never named Bobby Henderson, but she talked about how she fell in love for the first time in her life with a married pianist who had a couple of children, a man almost as old as her father. "It was the first time I was ever wooed, courted, chased after. He made me feel like a woman," she wrote. "He was patient and loving; he knew what I was scared about, and he knew how to smooth my fears away. But beyond that, no good could come of it. In fact, at one point I was taking it all so seriously it came mighty close to being tragic."

There's another version of that legend. It says that Billie was working at a club across the street. She sang with Bobby there, and then went to Pod's and Jerry's with him to audition. She was hired immediately. Billie liked the dramatic version of her audition tale.

As musicians, the two got off to a great start. The club owner offered Billie a steady job singing for a small salary, somewhere between twelve and eighteen dollars, plus tips, for six nights a week. Thrilled, she hurried to buy chicken and baked beans—her mother loved baked beans. And she gave the food and rent money to Sadie.

Billie regarded that job at Pod's and Jerry's, which paid her regularly, as her first professional work as a singer. At age eighteen, she was earning about fifty dollars a night—during the Depression, when other people were out of work and had to eat in soup kitchens so they wouldn't starve to death. She began to sing all over Harlem, getting to know the musicians. Benny Carter, who would become a famous alto saxophonist, composer, and arranger, heard Billie singing in a jam session in a club called the Bright Spot at 139th Street and Seventh Avenue even before she worked at Pod's and Jerry's. "I felt then that she had a touch of greatness in her," he would say for publication in a prizewinning book, *Lady Day: The Many Faces of Billie Holiday.*

Prohibition against liquor was still in force in 1933, and the law, which had to be changed by an amendment to the Constitution, wouldn't be repealed until December. Some clubs were closed down one night by police and reopened the next night under a new name. Many clubs, including Pod's and Jerry's, on 133rd Street near Seventh Avenue served drinks and did a lively business. Billie worked at Pod's and Jerry's with other young African-Americans who later became legendary figures in jazz and entertainment.

One writer discovered that Bobby Henderson wasn't married. He lived with his mother and was devoted to her. Engaged to Billie for a while, he became afraid of her moodiness and noisy arguments with her mother. Bobby had a weakness for alcohol, and he and Billie soon broke up.

She was part of a floor show that began with George "Pops" Foster, a bassist who had come up from New Orleans on the riverboats. He not only kept the rhythm by playing the bottom of the chords of songs, but he entertained by slapping his bass. That was a popular, old-fashioned gimmick. Dancer Charles "Honi" Coles, who became a famous tap dancer on Broadway in his later years, danced at the club. One of his protégés, a youngster named Baby Lawrence, a singer, learned to dance from Honi there. Baby Lawrence became a famous tap dancer, too.

Pops Foster later recalled that Billie had been a "stone hustler" until she realized how well she could sing. People loved her singing and threw big tips at her. Pops considered her the showstopper at Pod's and Jerry's. Irene Kitchings, a pianist and composer, saw Billie sing at the club. Kitchings thought Billie was a girlish, enthusiastic, friendly youngster. The crowd always wanted her to sing "Them There Eyes." Billie was a great singer of "bright tempos, the rhythm songs . . . what we called in those days the jump tunes," Kitchings recalled.

Other musicians in Harlem in the early 1930s heard Billie sing at an after-hours place called Goldgraben's and at the Ubangi Club, the Yeah Man Club, the Hot Cha, and Monette's, among other places. Not all of the musicians loved her style immediately. Some of them thought it sounded flat in spirit. It was not the lively style of singing they admired in Ethel Waters, whose voice sounded bell-like. Billie didn't have a powerful, loud voice like the famous blues singer, Bessie Smith, either. Bessie didn't need a microphone. It took a while for people to understand Billie's sensitive interpretations of emotion-filled songs.

Monette Moore, a singer, owned her own club on 139th Street. Most customers on the street were African-American. But

From a young age, Billie had admired the great blues singer Bessie Smith. But some people who heard Billie early in her career couldn't understand why Billie didn't sing more like Smith or Ethel Waters, who both had loud and powerful voices.

a few were white. Among them was a very unusual twenty-two-year-old man named John Hammond. A Yale graduate and a member of the Vanderbilt family, he could have relied on his family connections and spent his time making the rounds of fashionable parties and resorts. But he didn't want to live the life of a sheltered aristocrat and socialite. He had fallen in love with the blues and early jazz.

Bessie Smith was his ideal as a blues singer. He was producing records for Columbia, working with her and also with clarinetist Benny Goodman and others. These people would become legends in American music. A few years later, Hammond became a major promoter of Count Basie and his band. He brought the group out of a Kansas City club and sent them on tour. He helped the band win international fame and fortune. In 1933, John Hammond was writing a column about jazz for *Melody Maker*, a British magazine, and he often looked in Harlem clubs for musicians to write about.

One night he went to Monette's to hear Monette Moore. Instead, he heard a soft, enticing voice singing a risqué song: "Would'ja for a Big Red Apple?" It was the song of a girl asking a man to be her teacher in lovemaking. "If I had a big red apple, / Would'ja keep me after school?" Billie's voice caught his attention completely. She sang other songs, too, and made the rounds of the tables, picking up her tips in a way that was common practice at Harlem clubs then. The girls lifted their dresses and picked tips off the tables as best they could, with their legs and pelvises working together. A legend later arose that Billie got her nickname, Lady, at that time because she refused to pick up her tips that way. The truth was that she picked up her tips with her dress hiked up, too, as all the other girls did. She might not have liked it, but she had to do it or else pass up the tips and maybe even lose her job.

Billie also sang a blues number and another very sexy song. Hammond was actually embarrassed. But he thought her voice was wonderful—the best one he had heard since Bessie Smith's. He asked Monette who the singer was. Monette answered without enthusiasm, because she had wanted Hammond to pay attention to her. "That's Billie Halliday," Monette said.

Billie was using the last name Halliday because she liked the association with her father. Since he was a popular, well-known rhythm player in the jazz world, his name boosted her reputation. At the same time she didn't want to seem to be using his name outright and cashing in on it. So she altered the name a little to Halliday. It suggested her independence, her illegitimacy, and her relationship to the talented Clarence Holiday.

For the April 1933 issue of *Melody Maker*, Hammond wrote: "This month there has been a real find in the person of a singer named Billie Halliday. Although only eighteen, she weighs over two hundred pounds, is incredibly beautiful, and sings as well as anybody I ever heard." Another writer described her as "irresistible." Though Billie did weigh over 200 pounds, she was extremely tall, and she moved in a way that made her seem self-assured and fearless. With her poised demeanor, her pretty face, her glowing light complexion, and her regal bearing, she stood out in a crowd.

Hammond brought clarinetist Benny Goodman to Monette's to hear Billie and suggested that Benny record with Billie for Columbia. It didn't matter to Hammond that Billie was African-American and Goodman was white. Actually Hammond wanted to promote integration on the recordings he produced. He had already gotten Goodman to play in the background for a Bessie Smith recording. Goodman was persuaded to work with Billie, too. Though he worried a little in those days about the consequences of interracial recording dates, he later promoted integration in his groups. And his ear told him that Billie's voice was rather special. He also thought she was beautiful. Briefly, he joined the ranks of men with whom Billie had romances. And he agreed to work with her.

In the nine-piece group that Hammond assembled to be led by Goodman, the only African-Americans were Billie; trumpeter Shirley Clay, a man despite his feminine first name; and pianist Buck Washington, a member of a famous vaudeville team known as Buck and Bubbles. Billie had never before visited a recording studio, much less sung in one. She was quite nervous. Everybody was given a written part to play. Billie couldn't read music, and she knew that Washington couldn't, either. But he was an experienced performer, and he whispered encouragement to her. "You're not going to let these people think you're a square, are you?" he said. He didn't want her to look foolish in front of the white musicians. "Come on, sing it!"

The recordings didn't go down in history as her finest moments. She sang a song called "My Mother's Son-in-Law," on which her voice sounded girlish, strained, and high-pitched. When she heard it, she joked that it sounded like a comedy act. She recorded a second song with Goodman, too—"Riffin' the Scotch." Her voice sounded mellow on that one because she sang within her range. Her recordings heralded a new era of jazz singing, in which the art of improvisation combined with intimate feeling and emotional expressiveness, would become increasingly important. The very best singers were regarded as instruments in a group. Billie's approach to harmony, melody, and rhythm would have an enormous impact on most jazz and pop singers and many instrumentalists from then on. The power of her unique storytelling ability came from her feeling and her embellishment of the melodies. Most of all, her sound was earthy, musical, and a little strange. Nobody else could whine with such musicality. Most people thought she sounded like a soft-toned saxophone, but there was also a hint of a violin in her voice. That was a quality that helped give her voice such an odd timbre.

The recordings didn't make her an overnight star. For one thing, recordings done by African-American artists were called race records, and they usually weren't for sale in white communities. Billie kept struggling on the scene in the Harlem clubs and jam sessions. It was at a jam session that she met a tenor saxophonist named Lester Young. He had come to New York as a young hopeful. A few years later he joined the Fletcher Henderson band. That put him in the big time briefly. But his soft, subtle, modern sound didn't fit into an old-style, brassy big band easily then. He had to leave his job with Henderson.

The first time that Billie heard Lester play, she was attracted to his music. The excitement of his music was in his classy smoothness. They had so much in common—a lazy style that

This 1935 photograph from the film Symphony in Black: A Rhapsody of Negro Life *is one of the earliest known images of Billie Holiday as a singer.*

was laid back on the beat, a cool sound, and improvising talent that made their songs sound different every time they performed them. Lester taught Billie that one of her primary goals should be originality. She shouldn't sing a song the same way all the time. If she did, her art would degenerate into boredom. Most of all, Lester had a quiet, flowing style. He never blared or screeched on his horn. He always learned the lyrics to songs before he played them, so he would get the right feeling for them. He was especially sensitive to Billie's quietly swinging style and her treatment of lyrics. They became close friends quickly.

He visited her apartment. After Sadie heard him play, she sometimes thought that she was listening to Lester when it was actually Billie humming in a style very close to Lester's. There was a similarity in what they wanted to express. Like Billie, Lester had to withstand hard knocks and disappointments in his early life, and he would always suffer from insecurity about his status as an African-American man and a musician. He and Billie leaned on each other for warmth, reassurance, and support.

Whenever they met in a club, they were as excited as two puppies to see each other. "Lester knew how I used to love to have him come around and blow pretty solos behind me. So whenever he could, he'd come by the joints where I was singing, to hear me or sit in," Billie later recalled of their friendship. Lester started calling Sadie by the nickname "Duchess," and Billie became "Lady" and "Lady Day." To return the compliment, Billie dubbed him "Prez"—the President of the Tenor Saxophone. Everyone who knew them started using those nicknames. Eventually the press made them official in their articles and reviews.

By singing everywhere, Billie made her name better known. She was chosen to sing a blues song called "The Saddest Tale" with the Duke Ellington orchestra for a film called *Symphony in Black* in 1935. She was supposed to personify the blues and play the role of a luckless woman of the streets. That year, too, she made her debut at the Apollo Theatre on 125th Street. Somebody heard her singing in a club and got her a booking at the theater. The idea of walking out onto the Apollo's stage to face an audience that had a reputation for stunning performers with their screams of appreciation—or their hoots of rejection—frightened Billie. At the last moment in the wings, she turned to run out of the theater. The veteran comedian Pigmeat Markham, a bright star in the African-American entertainment world, noticed her distress. He pushed her out onstage. The audience loved her.

For that engagement, she called herself Billie Holiday. Her father by then was paying her some attention as a singer. He still didn't want to be closely associated with her in front of other people, however. When John Hammond mentioned her to Clarence, the guitarist tried to duck the relationship a little. He passed off his fatherhood lightly, saying it was just an accident that had happened as a result of virtually a one-night affair with

Sadie. Hammond was shocked and annoyed to hear Billie talked about so offhandedly. But a couple of musicians who worked with Clarence Holiday in Fletcher Henderson's band claimed that Clarence had actually used his influence to get Billie to perform with the band a few times. They had heard father and daughter sing together. And their vocal styles were similar. Both of them had a laid-back, ineffable rhythmic sense.

Clarence's wife, Fanny, told a writer years later that Clarence had actually tried to get Henderson to hire Billie, but Henderson didn't want to have relatives in the band. It's highly unlikely that Clarence ever championed his daughter to that extent. He surely never dreamed that Billie would become famous. It wasn't until she appeared at the Apollo for a second time that he became impressed with her growing success. She had done well enough to be invited back. He was proud of her.

His own career was in its heyday while hers was just beginning to build momentum. In 1933, he left the Henderson band, and he freelanced for a while. The next year he joined Benny Carter's band. In 1935, he may have worked with Bob Howard, a singer and pianist who, without great inspiration, imitated Fats Waller and had a regular show on CBS. Clarence also worked with Charlie Turner, a musician with a small reputation. And Clarence joined Louis Metcalf's band for a while. Billie may have sung with that band and toured with it to Canada, when her father played for it. In 1937, bandleader Don Redman hired Clarence—but not Billie. She was really always on her own. Her borrowed last name gave her more help than her father did directly.

BILLIE MAKES
CLASSIC RECORDINGS

Billie found a great supporter in John Hammond. He wanted her to do some recordings with Teddy Wilson, a pianist whose light, educated, articulate touch intrigued Hammond. Hammond had loved Wilson's clear playing on a radio broadcast in Chicago. So he had brought Wilson to record for Columbia in New York City. Billie had never heard of Teddy Wilson, but she accepted Hammond's invitation to go to Wilson's apartment and meet him.

That day the unsophisticated, friendly Billie and the extremely gifted Irene Kitchings, who was then Irene Wilson, Teddy's wife, became friends and mutual admirers. (Three years later Billie sang Irene's composition, "Some Other Spring," as well as several other Kitchings songs. Kitchings became one of the most important pioneering women pianists and composers in jazz.) When Teddy came home, he brought sheet music given to him by Hammond. Teddy and Billie were supposed to choose songs out of the pile and create very sophisticated recordings with their light touch and real jazz feeling. Hammond wanted the records to combine chamber music and jazz for intimate, swinging recording sessions.

Billie and Teddy were scheduled to record for Columbia's Brunswick label, without any budget to do second takes. They

Billie with musicians outside a Harlem nightclub

would have only one chance to get a record exactly right. Hammond had convinced the company's executives that they needed African-American versions of the hits that white musicians had done for the white market. But the executives weren't lavishing money on the players.

Billie and Wilson rehearsed in his apartment, so they could go into the studio and achieve the high standard that they wanted for the recordings. By rehearsing at home, without pay, they overcame the lack of a budget for more than one take in the studio. And they produced recordings that became classics of Billie's early years, and Teddy's, too. Some people consider those recordings the best of her career. Her voice was never clearer. At times it rivaled a bird's for purity.

Chosen for the first recording session on July 2, 1935, were Billie, Wilson, Benny Goodman, trumpeter Roy Eldridge, tenor saxophonist Ben Webster, drummer Cozy Cole, bassist John Kirby, and guitarist John Truehart. Each musician received fifty dollars without any possibility of royalties. Some of Billie's great up-tempo recordings that day were "I Wished on the Moon," "What a Little Moonlight Can Do," and "Miss Brown to You"—songs that she would sing throughout her career.

It was the start of a beautiful musical collaboration for Billie and Teddy Wilson. They often recorded together between 1935 and 1942. A brilliant accompanist, Wilson knew how to play fill-ins for her and not intrude upon her unique ideas for melodies. Later a girlfriend, singer Sylvia Syms, joked that Billie sang with such embellishments because she didn't really know the songs. But that was far from the truth. Billie understood the music so well that she was free to do anything with the melody. She eventually recorded hundreds of tunes for Columbia.

She was also offered the chance to start recording as a leader—Billie Holiday and Her Orchestra. That delighted her. In 1936, under her own name, she recorded "Billie's Blues." It has endured as one of the trademark songs of her career, about her man having left her again. She also did "Them There Eyes" that year. It became one of her most famous spirited interpretations. She had spent years singing it in clubs by then. With John Hammond, she chose the musicians for her groups. Among her favorites were trumpeter Buck Clayton and her buddy Lester Young, with whom she began recording in 1937. Like Wilson, the other musicians kept a careful eye on Billie so that their playing never overshadowed her role in the music.

Buck Clayton later recalled how he managed to enhance Billie's singing, both in the recording studios and later on the road with the famous Basie band. (Billie, Buck, and Lester toured with Basie beginning that year.) "Billie's pitch was in such a key that the trumpet player had to play high or low for her. Normally 'Body and Soul' was played in middle range, but with her you had to play high or low. If it were in the key of B-flat, Billie would sing it in F. And it was hard to play for her. She changed the original key; sometimes I would have to play it so high that the trumpet would screech. So then I would have to play it low. There was no middle ground with Billie.

"I would keep watching her mouth to see if she were fixing to close it. Then I'd fill in and play two or three notes until she was ready to sing again. Then I cooled it. That was the best way to play with Billie. I had more fun playing with her than with any of the [other singers] in the Basie band."

On the recordings, Buck sounded as if he loved playing for Billie. He played some of the prettiest and most arresting solos that any trumpeter ever played behind her.

Over the next few years, for Columbia, Billie sang many good songs—fine material to start with. Because occasionally she was given songs that were not first rate, some African-American musicians thought that she wasn't always given the best material because she wasn't white. But she always turned even the trite songs into pleasant interludes. The great songs became jazz classics. Among them were "The Way You Look Tonight," "Pennies from Heaven," "I Can't Give You Anything but Love," and, in February 1937, "Why Was I Born?" and "I Must Have That Man" with Buck and Lester in the band with Benny Goodman, Teddy Wilson, guitarist Freddie Green, and bassist Walter Page. All but Wilson later traveled with her in the Basie band. Other songs that she made memorable were "Let's Call the Whole Thing Off," "They Can't Take That Away from Me," "I'll Get By," "Mean to Me," "Easy Living," and "I'll Never Be the Same."

She was still a slightly known singer, better known in Harlem than in the rest of New York City or the country. The records gave her some exposure, but she still labored for her daily bread in such places as Clark Monroe's Uptown House, a downstairs club in Harlem. John Hammond took Count Basie there to hear her. Basie thought Billie was a pretty woman with a different sound. She could swing, too. Basie's band was a brassy, swinging, blues-based group. Yet he thought she could fit right in. Of course, he knew that Hammond, who was doing so much to promote the band, wanted Billie to work with it. So he welcomed her.

Just before she went on the road with Basie, something happened to shock her. She was singing at Clark Monroe's club when a telephone call came to her from Texas. Someone asked for "Eleanora Billie Holiday." Yes, Billie said. A voice on the other end of the line told her that her father had died while touring in that state. She was so surprised that she couldn't say anything. Clark Monroe took the phone and found out the details.

While touring with Don Redman in the South, Clarence had caught a bad cold. He needed to see a doctor, but there weren't any hospitals that would treat African-Americans in the area where he was traveling. So he waited until he got to a big city. By that time, he had pneumonia. The doctors couldn't do anything to save him.

Billie's relationship with her father had been both loving and resentful. He was her biological father, but she had never been able to get close to him. He never lived under the same roof with her. He had been a man of the world, a slick, charming, talented rhythm player who was here today and gone tomorrow. For Billie, he had been a virtual phantom. She had heard from other people about where he was playing and touring far more often than she had ever seen him. With his careless attitude, he had not bothered much about her existence. She had had just enough connection with him, however, to feel terrible about his death and to regret the end of her hope to get to know him better.

Billie thought that his lungs had been weakened by his bout with poison gas during World War I in Europe. That was unlikely. Actually he liked to drink, and he never took care of himself. He died a relatively young man, when he was still more popular in the jazz world than Billie was. He never lived to see the day when his career would be remembered only because of Billie's success.

The day of his funeral was one of the most confusing in her young life. At the service, before the trip to the cemetery, Sadie and Billie saw Fanny, Clarence's legal widow, and also one of Clarence's girlfriends, who had two children with her. Clarence was their father. The atmosphere was tense at the funeral service. Sadie wandered off and later said she had gotten lost on the way to the cemetery. Billie went there without her mother. That was Billie's last sight of the rambling man whose lifestyle had intrigued her and whose footsteps she had followed into music.

ON THE ROAD WITH
THE COUNT BASIE
AND ARTIE SHAW BANDS

Basie said that everybody loved Billie. He liked to call her William. That was his way of joking with her. His formal first name was William, and all his musicians called him Base or Bill. So Billie could be William. He paid her seventy dollars a week, a raise of thirty-five dollars over her salary at Clark Monroe's Uptown House.

Billie fit right in with the group of men on the bus. She did not require coddling. They could say anything in front of her. Buck Clayton later recalled: "She would shoot craps on the bus and be one of the boys and do things to help pass the time, so we wouldn't go crazy." She won some of the games. And she could smoke cigarettes and marijuana with those fellows who liked to smoke. She wasn't a heavy drinker, but she could drink steadily and keep up with the men. She loved to laugh and socialize. On the long overnight hauls, as the band bus raced through the darkened landscape, Billie, Buck, and Lester Young often sat up, talking with each other about life.

In many places where she sang with the band, Billie got wonderful reviews. *A History of the New York Jazz Scene* called her the "statuesque and effervescent Billie Holiday." The reviewer decided to stir up a little controversy by saying she

At The 125th STREET

APOLLO

AMERICA'S SMARTEST COLORED SHOWS!

THEATRE 125th Street Near 8th Av.

Telephone Un. 4-4490

ONE WEEK ONLY — Beg. FRIDAY, NOV. 5th

COUNT

BASIE

AND HIS NEW BAND

— with —

BILLIE HOLIDAY and JAS. RUSHING

AND A LEONARD HARPER REVUE CAST OF 50, with

BUTTERBEANS
and SUSIE

Monarchs of Laughter

3 MILLER BROS.

IN A NEW SPECTACULAR ACT

BIG TIME CRIP-HILDA ROGERS-PAUL BASS
JOHN MASON – JOHN VIGAL
"SADJI" – THE HARPERETTES

Deanna Durbin in "100 Men and a Girl"

| MIDNIGHT SHOW SATURDAY | AMATEUR NIGHT BROADCAST WED. |

MOTORISTS! COMPLY WITH TRAFFIC REGULATIONS!—Police Department, City of New York

In 1937 and 1938, Billie was the featured singer with the Count Basie band, which was the top-billed act wherever it played. This advertisement is for the Apollo Theatre in Harlem, New York, which is now considered a historical site of African-American culture.

was superior to Ella Fitzgerald. "There is more force, personality and sparkle in the Holiday voice than we ever noticed in Fitzgerald's, and that's going some." Ella Fitzgerald, with her sunny, cheery style, had already had a tremendous national hit with her novelty rhythm song, "A Tisket, a Tasket." News of Billie's success with Basie brought all the talented young musicians out to hear her at New York's Savoy Ballroom, a popular dance hall in Harlem. Billie was taped there singing with the band.

There were troubling racial incidents on the road. Billie and all the men in the band were African-Americans. In one club in Detroit she was asked to use makeup to make her face look darker. The club owners felt nervous about a beautiful light-skinned woman standing on a stage with a band composed of African-American men, most of them with darker complexions than hers. At that time, entertainers were segregated onstage. Billie had to do what the club owners asked.

One day in late fall of 1937, Buck Clayton woke up to find out that Billie was gone from the band. He couldn't figure out exactly why then, and he never really knew why. Rumors circulated. Basie had another singer, Jimmy Rushing, who performed the blues while Billie did the other songs—both up-tempo and slow dance numbers. Some people said that Basie wanted Billie to sing the blues, and Billie refused. But that didn't ring true to Buck. She sang anything that the band needed, although she didn't want to intrude on Rushing's territory. Rushing's vocals on the blues helped make Basie's band famous and popular.

The musicians didn't think that Billie was moody or inconsistent in her work habits. They believed that most audiences loved her. She didn't have a loud, brassy style. That was true. And Basie's band was famous for its big, exciting sound. But Billie could swing. She made the song "Swing, Brother, Swing" very stirring. She learned all of the Basie band's repertoire. It was never clear who fired her: Basie or John Hammond or the Willard Alexander Agency in New York, which was booking the band.

Clayton came to think that Billie's disappearance from the band had something to do with a never-explained disagreement between Billie and Basie, perhaps about money or about Billie's moodiness or inconsistency—problems that Buck had really never noticed. She did have a romance with one of the men in the band, guitarist Freddie Green. He was married and had children in New York. He never led her to believe that he would break up his marriage for her. And there was never any tension over the conditions of their relationship. Freddie was a steady fellow who never abused her. Successful singers usually found themselves the center of attention for men who wanted to take their hard-earned money. Freddie wasn't that type. Though she and Freddie had some fights, they weren't serious. Nobody paid much attention to them. And she and Freddie and almost all of the others in the band were good friends.

She may have been fired because she couldn't record with the band. She had a contract with Columbia, and Basie was recording for another company. Or perhaps she was fired because she didn't have wide enough appeal. Basie and the band loved her improvisations, but she did have an odd sound because of the unusual timbre of her voice and her relaxed phrasing—so slow and drawled with a subtle vibrato. The very thing that she was most famous for—laying back on the beat—would cause her the most grief commercially throughout her life. In the end, her style would rescue her from oblivion. She would never be forgotten. But in 1937, she didn't weather the Basie band's demands.

Willard Alexander of the booking agency had said a few unflattering words about Billie's attitude toward work. Some days she felt like working, and other days she didn't bother much; she was inconsistent. It's possible that Basie complained to Willard Alexander, and then the order may have come back from Alexander or most likely John Hammond to Basie's straw boss—a musician chosen from among the band members to make sure the band's operations ran smoothly. The straw boss probably told Billie she wouldn't be with the band anymore.

She told people in New York that she thought the firing was unfair. Basie never said he fired her, but he suggested that her pride and her belief in her unique musical style made the ups and downs, criticisms and snubs, in the entertainment world particularly difficult for her. She didn't hesitate to fight for what she wanted to do, because she didn't think anyone had the right or the knowledge to tell her how to sing. She was correct, of course. And if that was the reason she left the Basie band, it wasn't the first time that a fight about her singing style cost her a job.

Back in New York she worked hard to make a living. Whenever she was in town during her days with Basie, she had kept recording with her own band and with Teddy Wilson's group. Basie band players joined her orchestra in the studio when they were in town. And she played with Basie again at the Meadowbrook Lounge in New Jersey in November, after she was out of the band. That date was taped, though not formally recorded in a studio.

Not long afterward, she was hired by the white clarinetist Artie Shaw, who led a popular band. Everyone in his band was white, but Artie wanted Billie because he loved her singing more than anyone else's. He also hired a black drummer, Zutty Singleton, to help the band enliven its tempos.

Once again Billie had problems with recording dates, because she and Artie were under contract to different companies. Even more disturbing for her was some criticism that her sound didn't fit in with that of the Shaw band. The important critics loved her with Shaw, however. *Down Beat* said, in June 1938, "Her lilting vocals jibe beautifully with the Shaw style." But her sound was far more modern and artistic, with a timeless quality, different from any other band singer's. It bothered song pluggers, who wanted Shaw to play their companies' songs and get them airplay on the radio. Billie wasn't commercial enough. Shaw was pressured into hiring another singer, Helen Forrest, a white teenager who was very talented, too, and had a more familiar sound—a very good but less distinctive style— for audiences. She became an extremely popular band singer. Billie and Helen traveled with an uneasy truce between them at times, Billie suggested.

Not only artistic criticisms but racial harassment made Billie's life hell. At some dates, audiences were upset at the sight of a beautiful light-skinned woman singing with an all-white band.

Billie onstage at the Apollo Theatre in 1937

Billie had difficulty renting rooms in hotels where the band stayed; she couldn't eat or drink with the musicians in restaurants. She had to enter clubs by the back door. She wrote in her book about an incident in Boston: "The cats in the band flipped and said, 'If Lady doesn't go in the front door, the band doesn't go in at all.' [The club owners] caved in.

"Eating was a mess, sleeping was a problem, but the biggest drag of all was a simple little thing like finding a place to go to the bathroom. Sometimes we'd make a six-hundred-mile jump and only stop once. Then it would be a place where I couldn't get served, let alone crash the toilet without causing a scene. At first I used to be so ashamed. Then finally I just said to hell with it. When I had to go, I'd just ask the bus driver to stop and let me off at the side of the road. I'd rather go in the bushes than take a chance in the restaurants and towns."

The strain made her sick. She developed an inflammation of the bladder. For three months she suffered with it. First it was misdiagnosed as venereal disease by a doctor in the South. Then a specialist was called in Boston, and he cured her in a few days. But the racial slurs didn't stop. In one town a member of the audience called out "blackie." Billie swore at him, and the band had to leave town fast. Another time a white trumpet player took Lady Day for a friendly drink in a bar. Her presence provoked a fight with a white man there. He started kicking the trumpeter in the mouth. Billie and a maid working for the band pulled the musician free. Billie began to think of her days with the Basie band as a breeze.

She and Artie Shaw became close friends. A romance developed between them. Artie had Billie travel with him in his limousine, a Rolls-Royce, while the band went by bus. He liked to confide in Billie. And she understood his moods and the pressures on him; she could sense when he was feeling friendly or wanted to be left alone. "Sometimes he wanted to get lost on his farm without shaving for months, staying in this one pair of overalls, the way he did when he retired and wrote 'Back Bay Shuffle.' . . . I figured his moods were his business. He was like me, he didn't hurt anyone but himself," she later philosophized, telling it exactly the way it was, about her as well as about the bandleader. Shaw became famous for his eccentricities and his music. But she didn't like traveling in the Rolls-Royce, pretty as it was, because it wasn't built for the high speed necessary to cover the distance between gigs fast. She put up with the bumps, getting made into a milk shake, she said, only because Artie wanted her with him. And Billie worried that the other singer might be jealous. Life on the road was fraught with problems.

The end came when the band went to work in New York at a Midtown hotel that forced Lady to use the back door. She was very upset to find such discrimination in New York. Between shows, the hotel made her sit alone in a room upstairs. She couldn't even hear the music, which was broadcast on the radio, and the management cut down the number of songs she sang. "Finally, when they cut me off the air completely, I said to hell with it. I just fired myself. I told Artie he should have told me when the big wheels cracked down on him. . . . I had been with Artie a year and a half. We had had some real times. . . . There aren't many people who fought harder than Artie against the vicious people in the music business or the crummy side of second-class citizenship which eats at the guts of so many musicians. He didn't win. But he didn't lose either. It wasn't long after I left that he told them to shove it like I had."

Her romance with Artie Shaw ended then, too. Later, one of her accompanists, who came to know her well, surmised that Billie was hurt. She had hoped it would grow into a lasting relationship. Perhaps she was lucky, however. Artie's personal life was so complicated that he married and divorced more than half a dozen times.

BILLIE BECOMES A STAR
AT CAFE SOCIETY

John Hammond continued to stand by Billie. He took her to Greenwich Village to meet a man named Barney Josephson, who was setting out on a brave new enterprise in 1939. He was opening a club called Cafe Society Downtown at 2 Sheridan Square, in a neighborhood that was famous for attracting writers, artists, journalists, bohemians, intellectuals, and social revolutionaries. Josephson had run a shoe business in New Jersey, but he was throwing it over and opening a club where African-American entertainers could perform and mix with whites in the audience. It was a revolutionary advance in those days for whites and African-Americans to sit together in an audience. Segregation had never been legislated in New York or other northern states. But the races didn't usually mix in New York club audiences until Barney Josephson's club opened. Josephson liked the music that derived from the black culture, and he loved the principle that all men and women were created equal. His Jewish family had emigrated from Latvia in search of freedom, and he retained his sense of outrage over discrimination all his life.

Billie found Josephson and his workers cleaning and decorating his basement club. She was hired for opening night. As

Billie sings at the Cafe Society Downtown nightclub in 1939. In this photograph, the famous writer S. J. Perelman (wearing glasses) is seated at the front table.

the crowd of "celebrities, artists, rich society people" waited for the show to start, Barney, Billie, and everyone else connected with the club watched the door in suspense, hoping the cabaret license would arrive. Barney had only his liquor license in hand. The crew was getting panicky. At eleven o'clock, Billie used her sense of humor and her fearlessness and advised Barney, "Come on, let's take a chance. One night in jail isn't going to hurt anybody."

The license arrived at that moment, and the entertainers began—boogie-woogie pianists Meade Lux Lewis and the team of Albert Ammons and Pete Johnson, and the great blues shouter Joe Turner, who had begun his career in Kansas City a few years earlier and who wrote wonderfully racy songs. One was a blues number about a man who was so in love with a married woman that she could make his face turn cherry red from passion in her big brass bed. Billie came onstage next. The audience loved her distinctive, sophisticated, swinging style, with her subtle, creative embellishment of the melody.

Billie sang at Cafe Society Downtown for about two years, working seven nights a week, with no time off, for seventy-five dollars a week, she said. Barney Josephson said he paid her double that for a nine-month engagement. She had earned more, including tips, at Clark Monroe's Uptown House in Harlem. But Cafe Society Downtown, in a white neighborhood, was the turning point of her career. Everyone came to see her. Upper East Side socialites discovered her and became ardent fans. She had often met club owners, especially when she was on the road, who had disliked her odd sound and had yelled at her to sing faster and louder or get out. She had gotten out, but not before she told them to sing their way and she would sing her way. She had sometimes gotten into wild fights with them, too, throwing furniture and breaking things to make her point. Barney Josephson never criticized the way she sang. Anything she did onstage was all right with him.

At Cafe Society Downtown the first two acts of the night were bands. Then the singer was told to do three songs, get offstage, and come back to take her bows. Billie was also told to honor all her curtain calls. She should sing an extra song or even five songs—whatever the audience demanded. Billie always sang with one little spotlight on her face in a darkened room.

One night, as the applause started and the lights came up, she turned her back on the audience and lifted up her dress, showing her behind to the audience. Josephson knew that she liked to smoke marijuana; she sometimes left the club and took a turn around the block in a taxi, so she could smoke a joint. He didn't allow marijuana in the club. But he knew that she was often high and uninhibited at night. This night was no exception. He went backstage to ask her why she had lifted her skirt. She told Barney, to hell with that audience. Barney said, "What happened?" She said, "Don't bother me." So he figured it out. Billie must have heard someone in the audience make a remark about black performers and a mixed audience. "That kind of thing went on all the time," he said. By lifting her skirt, "Billie told them: 'You can kiss my black ass,'" Josephson deduced. "I didn't fire her. Of course I didn't fire her."

His sympathies were always with the underdog. He was a political liberal with socialist ideals, and he moved in leftist circles; his brother's Communist connections would eventually cost Barney Josephson dearly. But Cafe Society Downtown in the late 1930s and 1940s was a thriving club, featuring many of the best musicians and singers in the world. The great beauty Lena Horne later starred at his club and fascinated Barney and every other man who saw her. Barney had tremendous respect for Billie's gifts. He loved to watch her cast her spell over an audience.

One day a friend brought him a song with a strong message against lynching. The song was called "Strange Fruit," a metaphor for the bodies of lynched African-Americans hanging from trees in the South. The lyrics were powerful, and the music slow and dirgelike. Barney asked Billie to sing it.

She was wary of it, Barney noticed. She had never sung a message like that before, and she didn't know if she—or anyone—could put it across to a club audience. People came out to be entertained. The song would deliver a blow. No one could escape the song's stance against man's inhumanity to man. Some people would probably not accept it. She finally agreed to try it, however. On the first night, after she sang the song, she waited and worried about the dead silence in the club. One person finally started clapping tentatively. Then the whole audience joined in. Billie had brought it off.

She began to get requests for the song. From that time on, it was identified with her, and it constituted a complete break from her usual repertoire of blues, up-tempo songs, and love ballads. No other singer could perform "Strange Fruit" and find acceptance for it. She wanted to record it, but Columbia was leery. So she asked the executives to let her record it for a new little label, Commodore Records, which was being launched by Milt Gabler, a record store owner. Columbia agreed to let her

Billie recording "Strange Fruit"

do it. On April 20, 1939, Billie led her own orchestra for the recording session.

Though it was the most politically significant song she ever sang, it wasn't the only one she recorded that day. Among the others was a love song, "Fine and Mellow," which would always be associated with her. That was released on the flip side of the single record, "Strange Fruit." (Recordings were released as singles in those days. Long-playing albums didn't come on the scene until the 1950s.) During that recording session, Billie also recorded "Yesterdays" and "I Gotta Right to Sing the Blues." All her songs that day showed off a maturing Billie Holiday singing slow torch songs. Billie herself began to like her interpretations better. She came to think of "Strange Fruit" as a protest against the prejudice that had contributed to her father's death. "I'm a race woman," she explained.

In this period of her life, her voice was extremely clear, pretty, and haunting. At the end of the year she got together with many of her friends from the Basie band and recorded "The Man I Love," a lovely reverie. A few months later her recording of "Body and Soul" became a hit. "I'm Pulling Through" and "Laughing at Life" suited her perfectly. She always said that her songs reflected her personal life, and they sounded the way they did because she put her heart and soul into them. Cafe Society Downtown was turning out to be one of the best things that ever happened to her career, allowing her to enjoy consistent approval, a wider audience, and a steady paycheck. She was no longer the complete underdog, worrying about what awaited her around every turn in the road, in every club, and in front of each new audience.

She was still living in Harlem with her mother. Sadie wanted to open a restaurant. Billie gave her several hundred dollars that she had won by gambling on the Basie band bus. Sadie still didn't have enough money. However, Billie was attracting wealthy friends. One was an heiress who lived in her family's mansion on Fifth Avenue. She sent Billie presents, including masculine suits, which were strange presents for the feminine-looking Billie. The heiress, whom Billie called Brenda, visited Billie's apartment. Billie visited Brenda's house, too. Brenda idolized Billie. She had no other forthright, loving, or romantic relationships. Billie felt sorry for Brenda. People like Brenda were "incapable of loving anybody—just the opposite of my trouble," Billie said, analyzing her own character.

One day Brenda heard Sadie say how much she wanted to open a restaurant. Despite her emotional problems, Brenda was generous, and she gave Billie's mother the money. Sadie became the proprietor of her own soul food place, Mom Holiday's, on Columbus Avenue at Ninety-ninth Street on Manhattan's Upper West Side, in a white neighborhood close to Harlem. The restaurant immediately became a magnet for musicians, who enjoyed Sadie's good cooking. When they couldn't pay, she fed them for free at all hours of the day and night. Whenever Billie stopped there, her mother told her about financial problems. The Board of Health was always requiring Sadie to improve the place, or it would be closed down.

Billie wrote in her book, "The best paying customer she had was me." One day her mother told her that the Board of Health required the restaurant to have two toilets. Billie thought, "The damn Board of Health could pass by thousands of Harlem tenements with no damn toilets at all, then land on the Duchess and tell her she had to have two. So it would take a few hundred bucks for that. The next time I'd turn around, she'd say, 'The Board of Health was here again.'" Billie handed out fifty dollars for this, forty dollars for that. "I don't know how much it cost me to keep the Board of Health happy, but it was plenty. And I never got back a quarter. I only tried once. . . . I needed some money one night and I knew Mom was sure to have some. So I walked in the restaurant like a stockholder and asked. Mom turned me down flat. She wouldn't give me a cent. She was mad with me, and I was mad with her. We exchanged a few words. Then I said, 'God bless the child that's got his own,' and walked out."

Billie's disappointment in her mother for coming up so short and selfish led to one of Billie's major artistic achievements. She wrote the lyrics to a song called "God Bless the Child," about how her father might have money, and her mother might have, but God bless her if she had her own and did not ever have to ask for a penny.

> *Money, you've got lots of friends*
> *Crowding 'round your door,*
> *But when it's done*
> *And spending ends,*
> *They don't come no more.*
> *Rich relations give*
> *Crusts of bread and such.*
> *You can help yourself,*
> *But don't take too much.*
> *Mama may have, Papa may have,*
> *But God bless the child that's got his own,*
> *That's got his own.*

In that song Billie put into words one of the most important lessons she had ever learned. She was twenty-six years old when she understood and expressed how completely on her own she was and had always been. She had always hoped that her parents would give her stability and take care of her when she needed encouragement, support, and affection, but she had never been able to count on either of them. Now she had lost all of her illusions. It was her good fortune that she had learned to make her own way in the world. That was one thing that both her parents had taught her to do by their example, even if they had taught her rather accidentally. Both of them had always tried to improve their lives. Clarence had worked at music. Sadie had always looked for jobs, worked hard, and dreamed of a better life—a house, a restaurant, an elevated situation financially and emotionally. In these ways her parents had inspired her. But Billie was disappointed in Sadie when her mother began to feed off Billie's talent and not return the favor. The incident made Billie realize that whatever she gave herself, she would have. And nobody had ever really given her anything. There would be times when Sadie asked Billie for help of various kinds, and Billie would refuse. The relationship was complex, far from smooth. Billie had learned many good and bad lessons from Sadie.

Billie took her song downtown to composer Arthur Herzog, a friend of hers, who sat down at a piano and helped her pick out the music for her bittersweet lyrics. In May 1941, Billie recorded the song with pianist Eddie Heywood, Jr., and his orchestra, and with one of the greatest trumpeters of his era, Roy Eldridge, in the backup group. Known for his fiery style, he played tasteful, smooth accompaniment for her haunting message. The song became a classic and an emblem of her artistry.

During her years at Cafe Society Downtown, Billie kept gaining self-confidence and poise. Josephson thought it was because of his even-handed racial policies and the atmosphere of artistic freedom the club provided for her. Billie finally decided it was time to take a long vacation. Other talented African-

American singers followed her into Cafe Society and built their reputations.

A man named Joe Glaser, who left Willard Alexander's company and started his own, Associated Booking, was Billie's manager. She insisted that he find jobs for her that paid her more money than Cafe Society Downtown did. Glaser booked her into a club in California owned by Red Colonna, the brother of a well-known comedian, Jerry Colonna. At that club she began to find new friends and fans among the Hollywood stars. Comedienne Martha Raye, who could also sing jazz very well, came to hear her. When Billie was being heckled for singing "Strange Fruit," she thought she was going to lose her temper to the degree that she would have a fight with the young cracker in her audience. She was worried because she didn't have enough money in her pocket to get home to New York. Then Bob Hope, the comedian, jumped up onstage and heckled the heckler until he left the club. After Billie came offstage, she and Hope shared a bottle of champagne. As they were drinking, the building began to shake with one of California's fierce earthquakes. Billie joked about the effects of the champagne. Hope told her it was the worst earthquake he could remember.

Orson Welles, a great actor and director, also came to hear her. After becoming friends with her, he insisted that she guide him around Los Angeles's African-American community, particularly the clubs near Central Avenue. He was endlessly curious about the ghetto. Though she was bored with it, she liked him so much that she took him everyplace. Then she and Orson began to get hate calls, threatening both of them that they would never work again if they didn't stop seeing each other. They were just friends. That type of prejudice "makes life a continual drag," Billie reflected in her book. "Not only for me but for people I meet and like. You're always under pressure. You can fight it but you can't lick it." The only time she had escaped that kind of pressure, she reminisced, "was when I was a call girl as a kid and I had white men as my customers. Nobody gave us any trouble. People can forgive people any damn thing if they did it for money," she concluded.

One day when she was driving around with African-American singer Billy Daniels and his white girlfriend, their car broke down. Clark Gable, the most romantic figure among all of Hollywood's leading men, helped them fix it. He invited them for a drink in a country club, too.

On the whole, Billie took home wonderful memories of California. Even though she ended up without much money in her pocket and had to take a bus three thousand miles across the country, home to New York, she had met some good people and learned a few more makeup and wardrobe tricks. She had won loyal fans for herself on the West Coast, too.

S E V E N

A QUEEN AND A
HEROIN ADDICT
ON FIFTY-SECOND STREET

Billie moved around the country a great deal in the early
1940s. She was booked to go back into Cafe Society but
failed to show up. She sang often in Chicago. And she always
went home to New York, where she sang on West Fifty-second
Street between Fifth and Sixth Avenues. On that block a couple of dozen little jazz clubs had opened in the 1930s. At first
they were for whites only. Then Teddy Wilson and Billie found
jobs at a club called the Famous Door. Billie thought they were
the first African-Americans hired to perform in a Fifty-second
Street club. They were ordered not to socialize with the audience. Both Billie and Teddy were fired one night, she recalled,
after she sat down at a table with a wealthy young white man
named Charlie Barnet, a saxophonist who loved her singing
and begged her repeatedly to have a drink with him. She
broke the club's rule and took the consequences. Teddy was
fired, too, though he had done nothing wrong. Barnet, who
later became a well-known bandleader, helped Teddy get
another job.

In this period, Billie was becoming increasingly disappointed by her inability to become as commercially successful as
she thought she should be. She was earning about one hundred

seventy-five dollars a week on Fifty-second Street—a decent salary. But the money did not represent the degree of fame and fortune she was hoping for. She had not ranked in *Down Beat* magazine poll for singers yet, and she was sad that other singers, who imitated her, won instead. Ella Fitzgerald, who admired Billie, had patterned herself after the white singer Connie Boswell. Ella sang up-tempo songs all the time and became much more popular than Billie. It would not be until 1943 that Billie would win the Critics' Choice poll in *Esquire*, triumphing over Ella Fitzgerald and Mildred Bailey. Now Billie at least had prestige. In the 1940s she was always asked who her favorite singers were. Still, the respect was not the same thing to her as commercial success in record sales and consistent poll victories.

After being fired from the Fifty-second Street club, she was glad to get her old job back at Clark Monroe's Uptown House. In 1941, Clark Monroe's brother Jimmy, a hustler, came into her life. She had met him earlier, but it was not until this time that she started a romance with him. He had been married to an African-American actress, then had gone to England and returned with a pretty blond girlfriend, whom he "managed," as Billie described his relationship. But the English girl was not an entertainer; she was a prostitute, and Jimmy Monroe lived off her earnings. Billie was attracted to his slick manners and sharp-looking clothes. Her mother didn't like Jimmy Monroe and warned Billie that he would never marry her. Joe Glaser, her manager, also tried to discourage her from becoming involved with Monroe.

Billie was unable to see beyond Jimmy Monroe's attractive looks. She was earning enough money to entice Monroe, and he may have actually been infatuated with her. So she made up her mind. In September 1941, she and Monroe eloped to Elkton, Maryland. When they came back, Billie showed off her marriage license in front of her mother and Joe Glaser. But her victory was short-lived. Jimmy Monroe kept seeing other women. Billie thought one of them was the English girl.

One night, when he came home with lipstick on his shirt, Billie told him, "Don't explain. Take a bath." Once again, the pain of a rejection set her to writing a song. This one was about her husband's obvious infidelity and her continuing love for him. She knew her husband was to blame, and yet she tolerated his behavior and stayed with him. He didn't change; he kept running around. From childhood she had been conditioned to wait until someone had a few crumbs of time, affection, anything, to give her. And she had never learned to break off relations quickly with people who were completely wrapped up in themselves. Again, she took her lyrics to Arthur Herzog. By the time she recorded the song "Don't Explain" for the first time, in November 1944, Jimmy Monroe was long gone from her life. But he left her with a problem different from rejection—a problem with drugs.

At first she and Jimmy lived with her mother. Billie claimed she had been married a year before she began to notice that Jimmy had a habit of smoking opium. Billie was an old hand at smoking marijuana, but she had never smoked opium, from which heroin is derived. One night Jimmy became sick from his addiction. He began sweating profusely and suffering from chills and a fever. Sadie wanted to help him, but he told her to stay away from him. Billie stepped between them, and Jimmy hit her. Then the three of them got into a fight. Jimmy said he was leaving. Billie went with him, first to a hotel, then to an apartment. But they still weren't happy together.

Jimmy offered her some opium to smoke, and Billie accepted. She would always say that her troubled marriage and her new addiction to drugs had nothing to do with each other. She said it was her own decision to use drugs: "Jimmy was no more the cause of my doing what I did than my mother was. That goes for any man I ever knew. I was as strong, if not stronger, than any of them. And when it's that way, you can't blame anybody but yourself." But her dream of a happy marriage had vanished. The drug numbed the disappointment she felt about him.

Billie was performing at the Plantation Club in Los Angeles when Jimmy became involved in a business deal that made him

Billie singing at a Chicago nightclub in 1939

decide either to stay on the West Coast or to go to Mexico for a while. He and Billie separated. Sick because she was unable to find drugs for herself, Billie headed home to New York and lived in a little apartment near her mother's restaurant.

Billie didn't stay alone for long. She met a trumpeter named Joe Guy, a drug addict who injected heroin into his veins. Joe Guy could never be of any help to her. He needed her professional support far more than she needed his, and he was poison for her health. Too quickly Billie made the wrong decision and became involved with the young newcomer in town.

Sadie, who didn't want to live alone, was begging Billie to stay with her. Unable to cut all her losses and stand independent of all the people who were feeding off her, Billie kept numbing herself with heroin, injecting it into her veins now, and dividing her time between her mother's apartment and her own, where she lived with Joe Guy. And she and Joe made big plans. They didn't worry about their inexperience; they simply decided to organize a band and take it on the road. Loving the dream, ignoring the expense, Billie bought a big white bus, painted "Billie Holiday and Her Orchestra" on the side, and hired the musicians.

The first booking was at the Howard Theatre in Washington, D.C. On her way out of New York, Billie drove the bus to her mother's house, where Sadie fed everyone and hung curtains in the bus. Standing on the sidewalk, Sadie waved good-bye to Billie. "She looked like little Miss Five-by-Five with the most beautiful face you ever saw on a woman," Billie thought as she took a last glimpse of her mother that day.

As she was falling asleep in a hotel in Washington that night, Billie had a terrible premonition about her mother. She told Joe Guy, "You better be good to me, because you're all I've got now." Sure enough, when she got to the theater, she learned that her mother had died. She hurried to New York for the funeral, which Joe Glaser arranged. Billie changed her mother's clothes from a pink shroud to a good suit. "There wasn't anything else I could do," Billie thought. "Wherever

Billie Holiday in the 1940s

Mom was going, it couldn't be worse than what she'd known. . . . I went back to Washington and finished the week."

Billie's band was a losing proposition financially during those war years. She began doing USO tours. "I don't know how many miles I traveled singing to the troops during those years, by plane, train, even our own white bus." She tried dressing up and taking her pet dog, a boxer named Mister, with her on the army planes, but the conditions of travel were very rough on her. The planes were stripped inside, without any luxuries or comforts. In between such tours, she headed home to Fifty-second Street.

By this time, the little clubs there had relaxed their policy against hiring African-Americans and admitting them as customers. The club owners had discovered they couldn't ignore the financial rewards of integration. Billie was a star on the street, which nurtured many musicians in those years. Some, such as Dizzy Gillespie, would become world-famous. When he first played for Billie in a club, he became worried because Billie, who liked to sing behind the beat, didn't start singing at exactly the moment he had expected. He repeated his phrase and felt a tap on his shoulder. It was Billie. She said, "Don't worry about me. I'll be there." He marveled at how creatively she worked with rhythms.

She went back to California in 1942, where she played with her old friend, Lester Young, at a well-known jazz club, the Trouville. There she met Norman Granz, a university student who was running jam sessions at the club. He confided in Billie that one day he was going to be as important in jazz as John Hammond was. Billie liked Granz, who was then just a smart kid, she thought. She would record for him much later in life, when he had made good his promise and become one of the most important jazz concert promoters, artist managers, and record producers. His label, for which she recorded throughout the 1950s, was first called Clef, then Verve. So Billie was forging friendships in the 1940s and coming to the attention of all the people who would help jazz to ascend to its rightful status as one of the most important American-created arts. Her manager, Joe Glaser, also became a major figure in jazz history; he managed Louis Armstrong. Norman Granz started the Jazz at the Philharmonic concerts, an important series that existed for years, with the first concert featuring Nat "King" Cole in Los Angeles in 1944.

With the popular Paul Whiteman Orchestra in Los Angeles, in 1942, Billie recorded "Trav'lin' Light," which became one of her most famous and best-selling records. Then she returned to New York and spent the rest of the war years in the clubs on Fifty-second Street: Kelly's Stable, the Famous Door, and the Onyx, Downbeat, and Spotlite clubs. Because of a musicians' union strike against the recording companies, Billie made no recordings from the end of 1942 to the beginning of 1944. She was not a member of the union—singers didn't belong to it—but without the instrumentalists, who were striking to get royalties from their recordings, she had no one to play behind her in the studios.

However, she sang to live audiences. She performed in the first Esquire All-American Jazz Concert, which was recorded at the Metropolitan Opera House, on January 18, 1944, with Louis Armstrong, Roy Eldridge, trombonist Jack Teagarden, clarinetist Barney Bigard, tenor saxophonist Coleman Hawkins, pianist Art Tatum, guitarist Al Casey, bassist Oscar Pettiford, and drummer Big Sid Catlett—all of them among the greatest jazz players of their era. Like Billie, each one had been a winner in the Critics' Choice poll.

When the musicians' strike ended, she went back into the studios with Eddie Heywood and His Orchestra and sang some of the torchy love songs she emphasized by now: "My Old Flame," "I'll Get By," "I Cover the Waterfront," "I'll Be Seeing You," "Embraceable You," "As Time Goes By," and others, especially "I Love My Man" and "Billie's Blues." That was the first time she recorded "Billie's Blues" in a studio. It had been so well received at the Esquire concert that she decided to record it in a controlled setting.

The song "Lover Man" came to her attention at that time. She wanted to record it with strings, the way she insisted it should be done. Nobody wanted to do it that way with her.

*Billie performs at the Esquire All-American Jazz Concert
in 1944. At the piano is Art Tatum, one of the legendary
jazz pianists of all time.*

She finally persuaded Milt Gabler, who had recorded "Strange Fruit" for her, to do "Lover Man" in late October 1944. He had taken his little label, Commodore, into the bigger firm of Decca. "Lover Man" was the first recording that Lady Day—or any other jazz artist—had ever recorded with violins. It became a hit for her, and she was very proud of herself for doing it her way. She left Columbia and moved to Decca that year.

She recorded with a variety of orchestras in the studios, at theaters, and in concert halls. Her own band had not been able to survive financially. Joe Guy was still with her; he played trumpet for all her dates. Norman Granz had been true to his word and had launched the concert series known as Jazz at the Philharmonic. In April 1946, Billie sang with a jazz orchestra that included Buck Clayton and probably Lester Young, in a Jazz at the Philharmonic concert at the Embassy Theater in Los Angeles. Because she was working in a club in Hollywood, that was a convenient time for her to make a film. Joe Glaser found her a role in New Orleans.

Billie was excited about making a movie—until she discovered that she had the role of a maid. All she said was "Yes, Miss Marylee" and "No, Miss Marylee" countless times. She tried to get out of the job, but the contract was signed. She sang for the movie, and so did Louis Armstrong. But the day came when she couldn't stand to say "Yes" and "No, Miss Marylee" anymore, and she actually burst into tears on the set. Soon the job was over. Her satisfaction came the next year, when the movie received terrible reviews. Only her brief moments of singing for the sound track were praised by the critics.

Again she returned to New York. Usually she could be found in the Fifty-second Street clubs, for which her style was perfectly suited. The big band era was ending, and small groups with an intimate sound were becoming popular. Billie was a star on Fifty-second Street. But sometimes she was too sick from heroin to show up for her shows. She was becoming notorious for her unreliability in the music world, where everyone knew what everyone else was doing.

Sylvia Syms, then a teenager aspiring to be a singer, was in Billie's dressing room one night when Billie was getting ready

In this 1945 promotional photograph, the strain and trouble in Billie's personal life is evident in her expression.

to go onstage. Billie was using a curling iron on her hair. She was so high on heroin that, without realizing what she was doing, she burned a hunk of her hair. Sylvia did some quick thinking. She went out and bought a gardenia to cover the damaged spot in Billie's hair. Billie had worn flowers in her hair before, but that night marked the time when she adopted a white gardenia as a trademark. "I had the white gowns and the white shoes. And every night they'd bring me the white gardenias and the white junk," Billie wrote.

One night in a club she began to slow a song down so much that her accompanist, Joe Springer, was worried she might drop out altogether. He didn't know what to do. Heroin had completely befuddled her. She was barely able to stand up. Then suddenly she skipped a lot of words and caught up with him. Somehow she had managed to keep track of the music, though she had been falling asleep on her feet. She had awakened in the nick of time.

She called herself a slave to heroin. She was earning about a quarter of a million dollars a year, and about a quarter of that went to maintain her habit. She may have spent as much as five hundred dollars a week, which would be equal to thousands of dollars now. So she decided to try to quit using the drug. She told Joe Glaser what she wanted to do. He arranged for her to go into a clinic in New York for three weeks. Tony Golucci, the owner of the Famous Door, where she was working at the time, offered to help her, too, in any way she needed.

With the moral and practical support of her friends, she weaned herself away from heroin at the clinic. She thought that the whole matter would be kept strictly confidential. But when Joe Glaser's secretary came to pick her up at the end of treatment, Billie noticed she was being followed by a policeman. Billie never found out who had told the police about her addiction. She thought it might have been somebody who worked at the clinic. The police put pressure on the clinics to turn over information, Billie believed. All she knew for sure was that, before she went there, she had never seen the police come near her. Now they were watching her.

EIGHT

A LONG, HARD JOURNEY
TO CARNEGIE HALL

In late 1946, just before Billie went into the sanitarium, she was booked to play in the Downbeat club, singing with Eddie Heywood's sextet. But he had become famous on his own, and his management didn't want him to give the spotlight to Billie. Furthermore Billie's reputation for being erratic handicapped her. She made some accompanists nervous.

When she showed up for work on opening night, she didn't have an accompanist. Her friend Tony Scott, a clarinetist, went for a walk on Fifty-second Street and sighted a young pianist named Bobby Tucker. Just out of the army, Bobby was working as an accompanist for another singer. That night, however, he was free. Tony Scott asked him to go into the Downbeat and play for Billie.

Naturally, Bobby was worried about going to work without any rehearsal. But he decided to try it. He knew the songs from listening to the records Billie had made with Teddy Wilson; Bobby had played them for fun. "She hired me in the middle of the [show]," he later told John Chilton, author of a book called Billie's Blues. "From that first show till she died, we were the best of friends."

Another writer, Robert O'Meally, found out, however, that

Bobby didn't love Billie's singing right away. He thought her sound was rather "flat," and he preferred Ella Fitzgerald's great rhythm singing and Sarah Vaughan's beautiful voice. Tony Scott explained Billie's genius to Bobby: "A singer like Ella says, 'My man's left me' and you think the guy went down the street for a loaf of bread or something. But when Lady says, 'My man's gone' or 'My man's left me,' man, you can see the guy going down the street. His bags are packed, and he ain't never coming back. I mean like never." And Bobby understood that Billie had no rival in communicating feeling. "I started listening to what she was saying and how she was saying. And once you start that, you can't get away from it."

Bobby's only bad habit was smoking regular cigarettes, and he eventually gave them up. He was an enormously talented, strong pianist with very close ties to his family in Morristown, New Jersey. His attitude toward Billie, who had struggled successfully against her addiction, was very tolerant and kind. When she came out of the clinic, Bobby took her to his mother's house so that Billie could take extra time to recover away from the glare of publicity. But when Billie returned to sing in a club on Fifty-second Street, the drug sellers flocked to her. She had pre-performance jitters. The temptation was too great. Soon she was injecting herself with heroin again.

In the spring of 1947, she went to play at the Earle Theater in Philadelphia. As she was returning after the show to her hotel on the last day of her engagement, she saw police cars parked outside. She didn't know exactly what was going on. The police were raiding her room. Sensing trouble, she, her chauffeur, and her dog, Mister, drove back to New York City right away. There, she started an engagement at the Onyx Club on West Fifty-second Street. And she and her manager, Joe Glaser, talked about what she should do. The police wanted her in Philadelphia. If she went back and faced them, Glaser said, he could try to use his influence to save her from a prison sentence. She would have to sign herself into a rehabilitation center again, he said. The government might cover the expense.

Throughout her career, Billie (in hat) was daunted by comparisons to the popular jazz singer Ella Fitzgerald (second from right).

Before she went back to Philadelphia, the police in New York went to her hotel and arrested her boyfriend, Joe Guy. Billie saw that she would have no peace. She went back to Philadelphia to face charges of possessing and transporting narcotics. The judge at the trial was told that Billie was the victim of parasites—the drug sellers. They dogged her steps and charged her one hundred dollars for doses of heroin worth about five dollars. She had become so handicapped by heroin that, in the year prior to her trial, she had earned only about $56,000. She really had no money left. The judge thought she was pathetic, but he told her that he had to regard her as a criminal defendant. He sentenced her to a year and a day in the Federal Reformatory for Women at Alderson, West Virginia. She was shocked and miserable.

First she was taken off drugs cold turkey, with none of the comforts and aids she had experienced in the New York clinic. Then she was given physical and mental tests and sent to work in the vegetable fields. (The prison raised all of its own food.) One day she collapsed from the heat of the sun because she wasn't used to farm labor. The doctor told the prison authorities to give her another job because she was a city girl. At first they assigned her to herd the pigs, a job she detested. One day she fell asleep on a pigsty roof. The prison officials thought she had tried to escape. When she woke up, she was put in solitary confinement for a few days. Again the doctor rescued her. She was assigned to work in the kitchen of the cottage where she stayed.

The job was called Cinderella, because she had to prepare and serve all the food to the other women, then carry twelve buckets of coal every day. Although the prison counted every morsel of food—every carrot—Billie tried to get extra food for some of the women, especially those who had been drug addicts. She knew how hungry they could feel immediately after they stopped using drugs. She also made the coffee strong, and she ran through coffee faster than the prison authorities approved of. For Christmas she tried to make whiskey out of potato peels. When the brew started to ferment, the odor permeated the whole cottage. The warden found the whiskey and threw it out.

Her time in prison was grim. When the door to her cottage was slammed shut at night, the sound reminded her of the Catholic institution she had been sent to in Baltimore. Now she was allowed to receive letters only from her immediate family. But the members of Billie's immediate family—her mother and father—were dead. She had no idea where she could find her half brother and half sister by Clarence and his girlfriend. Eventually, the prison officials allowed her to receive a few letters a week. She learned that people had been writing to her all the time. "During the months in the joint, they told me I was receiving packs of mail every day. It gave me a terrific kick to know people remembered me. At Christmas time especially I got over three thousand cards from every state in the Union and from towns like Shanghai [China], Bombay [India], Cape Town [South Africa], and Alexandria [Egypt], as well as all over Europe."

A couple in Switzerland sent her a thousand dollars and telephoned to invite her to live with them when she got out of jail. They told her they were worried about how people would regard her and how she would deal with life then. "I think I can make it," she told them. The warden, whom Billie liked, let her stay in contact with Joe Glaser, Bobby Tucker, and a man who wanted to replace Glaser as Billie's agent. The warden wanted Billie to have an easy time making a career comeback when she finished her jail term. "The warden was a real nice chick. She was a fine woman," Billie later reflected. The warden brought flowers to women when they were feeling most sad.

Billie was so depressed by the jail that she didn't sing a note during her entire sentence. "I didn't feel like singing," she wrote. "So I didn't. A lot of the girls in there were nice kids. They used to beg me to perform, and they'd get sore at me when I refused. It didn't matter. I couldn't have sung if I'd wanted to. If they'd understood my kind of singing, they'd have known I couldn't sing in a place like that. The whole basis of my singing is feeling. Unless I feel something, I can't sing. In the whole time I was there, I didn't feel a thing."

After eight months passed, she was set free. In Alderson, West Virginia, there was nothing but the prison. She knew that anyone who saw her waiting for the train would know right away that she had just gotten out of prison. It didn't matter that she was wearing a mink coat. She felt embarrassed, but she was also thrilled to be free. She took the train to Newark, New Jersey, where faithful Bobby Tucker met her, bringing along her dog, Mister. Billie had changed trains in Washington, D.C. where she had made a connection. She had actually bought drugs and gotten high. Bobby Tucker said, "Lady, how could you?" That was all he said, he told Donald Clarke, the author of *Wishing on the Moon*, a very vivid biography of Billie. Bobby didn't desert her. The boxer was so happy to see her that he knocked her hat off and pushed her over. He was licking her face. She would never forget his welcome. She was about to get a very excited reception from many people, too—though not from everybody.

Bobby took her to his mother's farm in Morristown. The house was being painted; his piano was on the porch. Billie was scared that she wouldn't be able to sing anymore. Bobby didn't want her to wait a minute longer and become even more afraid. He sat down on the porch and played "Night and Day." Billie started singing. "I'll never forget that first note, or the second," she wrote. "Or especially the third one, when I had to hit 'day' and hold it. I hit it and held it and it sounded better than ever. Bobby almost fell off the stool, he was so happy. And his mother came running out of the house and took me in her arms," Billie wrote in her book.

She was rehearsing for a concert at Carnegie Hall scheduled for ten days after she got out of jail. All of the musicians in her group went to Bobby's house to rehearse with her. Only a few items announcing the concert were placed in the newspapers, but it was sold out quickly. The Carnegie Hall staff had to place three hundred seats onstage to accommodate some of the audience. Billie, dressed in a black gown with short sleeves and a graceful floor-length skirt and long white gloves, was surprised to see the people onstage. At first she thought they belonged to a choir.

The first set she sang was an overwhelming success. Somebody sent her a bouquet of white gardenias for good luck. During intermission, before the second set, she took the flowers out of their box and fastened some to the waistline of her dress and more to her hair. By accident a hatpin sticking out of a bunch punctured her scalp. She was so excited by the concert and the cheering audience that she didn't notice how much she was bleeding. The blood began running down her face. Bobby Tucker was alarmed. He screamed, "Lady, you

*Despite her troubles offstage, Billie had grown to be
the idol of countless fans in the late 1940s.*

can't go on, you must be dying!" The wife of her bassist, John Levy, helped put ice packs on Billie's head to stop the bleeding. "She was bleeding heavily," John Levy remembered. The blood-stains didn't show on her black dress. But the accident on top of the excitement made her feel weak. She cut out only one song, "Night and Day," of the thirty-three songs she had planned to sing. Afterward, she had the strength to take only a few curtain calls.

That concert on March 27, 1948, was a critical triumph. The glamorous audience came from Harlem, Greenwich Village, the Fifty-second Street clubs, and the Park Avenue mansions. *Down Beat* reported that the ovations for Billie were thunderous. *Time* called the applause "hysterical." The show business newspaper, *Variety*, said, "A year hasn't dimmed her popularity or skill." Billie received $2,500 for the concert—a little more than a third of the price of all the tickets sold. Best of all, despite the accident, Billie felt as wonderful as she looked and sounded. She said the concert was the greatest thing that had ever happened to her.

NEW COMPLICATIONS

T hen, Billie found out, "came the terrific letdown." Because she had been convicted of a crime, she was no longer eligible to have a cabaret card in New York City. It would take many years for that law to change. Billie could play in theaters and concert halls, on television and on radio, but not in clubs or cabarets. And those were the places where she had always done most of her work in New York.

Billie tried to get around the handicap by working in a show called Holiday on Broadway. It opened at the Mansfield Theater on April 27, 1948. She received wonderful reviews, and she was amused by all of the details of her Broadway stardom. The lights turned the drums purple. The drummer's sticks glittered yellow. Billie took five curtain calls on opening night. She was heartened and thought she would manage to rebuild her career. But the show closed after three weeks. She was not a Broadway actress; she was a jazz singer who was meant to star in intimate clubs.

So she went back on the road—first to a club in Philadelphia, where she was shocked to see the warden from Alderson in the audience. The warden had quit her job and had come to the club to cheer Billie on. Billie went on to

Washington, Boston, and San Francisco. Back in New York, she still couldn't find anyone willing to hire her without a cabaret card and run the risk of having a club shut down. Then she was introduced to a man named John Levy, who seemed to be the boss of the Ebony Club on Fifty-second Street. This John Levy was no relation to her bassist, who had the same name. She never figured out exactly whom Levy of the Ebony Club was working for. He promised her that she could sing there, and the police wouldn't bother her.

Terrified that she would be arrested in the middle of a song, Billie nevertheless decided to take Levy's invitation to try to work in a New York club again. Bobby Tucker and his group, including bassist John Levy, supported her. The Latin bandleader Noro Morales alternated sets with Billie. And sure enough, the police left Billie alone. Every night the club was packed with customers. Billie deduced that somebody backing Levy's club had paid off the police.

Levy bought Billie expensive gowns and jewelry. He also let her draw a little money for her personal use. He handled all of the money for the group, and the musicians began to miss some of their pay. Billie never asked for an accounting. She was actually afraid that she might discover she owed him money, because her salary might not cover the beautiful things he was buying for her.

Billie had moved into a hotel after leaving Bobby Tucker's farm. John Levy then found her a beautiful, completely furnished apartment and said it was hers. Billie began to get the idea that John Levy was trying to start a romance with her. Both her husband and Joe Guy were gone from her life. And she was right. After a little while more, John Levy presented her with a house in Saint Albans, Queens, a quiet residential neighborhood. Saint Albans was beginning to fill with well-to-do African-Americans. "I even began to catch myself thinking I might be happy one day again. That, as usual, was fatal," Billie wrote in her autobiography.

Levy persuaded Billie to use him as her manager and edge Joe Glaser out of her life. In 1949, after Billie's long run at the Ebony Club, Levy booked her into the Strand Theater on Broadway for $3,500 a week for eight weeks. She performed five shows a day, seven days a week. All she saw was the inside of her dressing room. She asked Levy for some of the money she was earning, but he refused to give her any. He said that she had a car, a chauffeur, and charge accounts everyplace. What did she need money for? She wanted to pick up some of the lunch bills when she ate with friends in restaurants near the theater. But she could never treat them. Billie felt trapped and afraid.

She started to think about her hard luck. Some people wished her well, she knew, and hoped she would succeed more than ever, and some people watched to see if she would take a wrong step. She began to worry that crowds were coming to her performances because they hoped she would fall on her face.

The popular singer Peggy Lee, who also wrote fine songs, invited Billie to a party at a well-known Fifty-second Street jazz club called Bop City. Peggy gave Billie a song she had written in Billie's honor. At just that moment another guest made a remark about Billie's past. All of the other guests froze. The conversation stopped dead. Billie was humiliated.

Billie was having a hard time in general living down her reputation. Some people talked to her; some didn't; some insulted her. After finishing her engagement at the Strand, she was sent on the road with a band. Levy, who backed the show, still held on to all the money while Billie and her musicians did all the work. By then she was having an affair with Levy, but she wasn't enjoying life. Once again a parasite was taking all her money.

The bassist named John Levy had stayed with Billie while the group performed on Broadway, played off Broadway, and toured the country. He got as far as Philadelphia and decided to quit because John Levy, Billie's lover, wasn't paying the musicians. (Because Billie's lover and the bassist had the same name, the bassist was mistaken for the rest of his life for Billie's dishonest lover—an accident that irritated the bassist. The bassist went on to become an important manager for other musicians, including singers Joe Williams and Nancy Wilson and saxophonist Cannonball Adderley.)

Even Bobby Tucker decided to quit playing for Billie, because Bobby came to distrust and detest Billie's lover. Bobby later reflected, "I told Billie that I could line up a platoon of men in front of her and, blindfolded, she could pick out the two lemons." Bobby thought Billie's lover could qualify as two lemons all by himself. It was a sad day for Lady Day when Bobby Tucker, her loyal friend, felt pressured to leave her group. He found another job right away, with singer Billy Eckstine, and that collaboration lasted for more than thirty years.

A handsome man, Billy Eckstine became one of the most popular romantic singers in the country in the 1950s—and one of the first African-Americans in the music industry to thrill white audiences. When he was in his seventies and his beautiful baritone voice faltered, Bobby Tucker kept playing the piano, leading groups behind Billy Eckstine, and putting on a glorious show to support his boss and hide his frailties. Occasionally, Bobby Tucker still played for Billie in years to come, too. Their friendship endured.

Something very strange happened to Billie when she went to perform at a club in San Francisco. Levy, who was traveling with her, left her to go to Los Angeles on business for a few days. She took him to the train station in her beautiful white Lincoln with a red leather backseat that converted to a bed. The car had a bar and a telephone, too. She picked him up a few days later. Right away he started arguing with her. When they got to their hotel room, a phone call came for him. He handed Billie a package and asked her to flush it down the toilet. Someone knocked on the door. At just the moment when Billie was heading to the bathroom with the package, Levy let four white men into the room. She and Levy were arrested for possession of cocaine. That was what was in the package that Levy had asked her to get rid of for him.

Because of her record, she seemed guilty to the police. Levy didn't use drugs. Billie was actually drug-free at the time,

Billie with Count Basie (left) and Billy Eckstine

Billie is booked at a San Francisco police station after her drug-related arrest in 1949.

too. She may have been sniffing drugs but not mainlining at that time. Newspaper reporters kept taking her picture with Levy when they came out of the police station where they had been booked. "Without those pictures, a lot of people might never know that he was a Negro," Billie later wrote. Joe Tenner, who owned the club where Billie was working, got Billie and Levy out of jail on bail for five hundred dollars each.

Billie went back to work at the club and told Levy that she would take all the blame for the cocaine arrest. He had no record; she did. Levy agreed to her plan and left the hotel. She moved into the home of friends—a doctor and his wife—in San Francisco. Someone in their social circle came up with the bright idea to have Billie check into a sanitarium and let the staff observe her. In twelve hours the professionals could determine whether Billie was lying or not when she said she wasn't using drugs. So Billie did that. After four days at a cost of a thousand dollars, the staff swore that Billie was clean and innocent.

With that testimony in her favor, Billie then had to convince a court that someone else had possessed the drugs and tried to frame her. The crime she was accused of was possession—not use—of drugs. Billie's friends found a highly respected criminal lawyer, Jake Ehrlich, to take her case. He asked her if she had ever seen the man who headed the team of policemen who had come to the hotel room and arrested her. "Sure," Billie said. She had seen him with John Levy at the Ebony Club. Levy and the man had let the club's photographer take a picture of them together. The man was supposedly a top investigator of the narcotics squad. When the lawyer heard that, he was thrilled—because he could prove there was some kind of plot behind the scenes, and Billie was being victimized.

It seemed plain that Levy was feeding the narcotics investigator information, framing people, and probably earning money in that way. At the time the police had come into their hotel room, Levy and Billie had been fighting about money. Billie went on trial in San Francisco, scared to death, and told her story to the judge and jury: "I'd been in trouble before. Two years ago I volunteered for the narcotics cure. . . . I ain't had no drugs since. I came home and society took me back. Thank God for allowing me my second chance."

The jury delivered the verdict: "Not guilty."

People cheered for Billie in the courtroom. John Levy telephoned to congratulate her. But it was Joe Tenner, the club owner, who gave her money to go back to New York. She owed money to the lawyer and to several other people. Months had elapsed between the day of her arrest and the day she was free to go home with a clean slate to New York. Her stay in San Francisco had been very expensive. She arranged to pay people back a little at a time. When people later asked her for the inside story of what had really happened, she said, "I wish I knew it myself."

She had to honor the bookings that Levy had signed contracts for. Avoiding him, she moved into the Hotel Henry on Forty-fourth Street—alone. Over the next few years she extricated herself from his clutches. His bookings had no special plan to build up her image or commercial prospects. In part, because she couldn't get a cabaret card to perform in New York City, her career became a slapdash, unorganized schedule of dates around the country and in Canada. Her recording contract with Decca—the first one she had ever had that paid her royalties—ended. She made some recordings for a little firm called Aladdin in the early 1950s. But she didn't have a well-planned recording schedule or a marketing plan for her recordings with any company.

In 1950, a *Down Beat* writer did her the dishonor of calling her Lady Yesterday. Billie had already felt hurt and disappointed because she had never won any of the popularity polls for singers in that magazine. Singers who admired and copied her were winning the polls. Jazz critics recognized Billie as a mistress of her art. They asked her which young singers she thought sounded good. Praise from Billie meant a great deal to the singers. One time she mentioned Perry Como and Jo Stafford. Another time she selected a group that included Etta Jones. "You always think your idol doesn't even hear you," Etta said, revealing her reverence for Billie. Carmen McRae, who had adored and learned from Billie for years, was about to become a jazz singing star who would rank in the popularity polls. She would tie with Ella Fitzgerald in the early 1950s. But Billie kept her head above water only because her fans loved her.

By 1951, she was back with Joe Glaser as her manager. Unhampered by John Levy, Glaser arranged for a bandleader to be her road manager. But Billie had a fight with him on the road. She asked her girlfriend Maely Dufty, whom she had met in New York, to travel with her as her road manager. Maely was no stranger to the jazz world. She had managed Charlie Parker, the legendary alto saxophonist, for a little while. Billie, who had no man in her life at the time Maely started working for her, swore to herself that she would never again become involved in a complicated relationship with a man. She wanted to take care of herself and keep life simple. Happy to have a girlfriend to travel with, Billie headed to Detroit's Club Juana.

A NEW HUSBAND,
A FINE RECORDING COMPANY,
A GREAT TRIP—
AND A BAD, OLD PROBLEM

A ll her resolutions against a new romance were abandoned in Detroit. A sharp-looking, fast-talking hustler named Louis McKay came to hear her sing. Billie had met Louis McKay for the first time in a Harlem club, the Hot Cha, when she was only sixteen years old. She liked to say that Louis fell asleep at the Hot Cha's bar, where a pickpocket was getting ready to steal his wallet. Billie woke Louis up and saved him from being robbed. She had not failed to notice that he was a very handsome young man. She was a pretty, healthy-looking girl herself.

Louis McKay started coming to the club in Detroit every night. If he came late, she cried. After that happened several times, she knew she was in love with him, and she made up her mind to get a divorce from Jimmy Monroe so that she would be free to marry Louis McKay one day.

There was another thing that Billie had made up her mind about, but she went back on her word. She started using heroin again. It happened between the time she and John Levy broke up their relationship in San Francisco and the night she met Louis McKay again, in Detroit. Some people would say that Louis McKay was just another hustler. But there were also many people who knew Louis McKay and thought that he really loved

Billie with Louis McKay

Billie and wanted to help her. He didn't use heroin. He wanted to see her quit using drugs. He worked for several years toward that goal, though he knew the odds were against him. Billie had spent too many years suffering through hard knocks, when real friends turned out to be few and far between.

She herself tried to explain the cause of her weakness. When she left jail in West Virginia, the prison authorities had offered her heroin to see if she was really cured. "I found I didn't want any, and that was a great kick. But with all the doctors, nurses and equipment, they never get near your insides at what's really eating you," Billie wrote in her autobiography.

Louis McKay and Billie rented an apartment in Flushing, Queens. Romantic daydreams welled up in Billie. She told reporters that she wanted to be a housewife and have children. She dreamed of adopting homeless children whom nobody wanted. She wanted to feed them and make sure they went to school, to punish them when they needed it, and to love them whether they were good or bad. She reflected that her mother, Sadie, had taken care of her as best she could. "But she was only a kid herself," Billie wrote, excusing her mother for all her shortcomings.

Billie also wanted to own a little jazz club where she could sing whenever and whatever she wanted to, the way she wanted to. She knew that a small club in New York was the ideal setting for her. She still pined for a cabaret card. And she knew how well she could still sing lyrics. "I've been told that nobody sings the word 'hunger' like I do. Or the word 'love,'" she said. After drifting around in life in so many ways, she was now feeling proud of herself.

In 1952, with Louis McKay to encourage her, she signed a new recording contract with a company called Clef, which would become Verve. It was owned by her old friend Norman Granz, now a powerful, influential jazz producer. First Billie Holiday, then Ella Fitzgerald, and then Sarah Vaughan, three of the most important jazz singers who ever lived, recorded for his label. Billie began recording some of her old hits for Granz's label. Her voice, which was beginning to sound a little raspy and weathered, seemed even more affecting to many fans. She was still in demand.

She kept touring the country to such important jazz clubs as Storyville in Boston, where the owner, George Wein, found that she was always nice to him. "I always treated her with respect, and I never had any problems with her," he would always remember. He was very amused when he took her out for a lobster dinner one night at Durgin Park, one of the most popular restaurants in town at that time, and she asked for a female lobster.

Billie and Louis McKay occasionally had fights. They were noisy and sometimes ended up with one or both of them getting hit and bruised. Billie actually liked Louis to hit her before she went onstage to put her in the right mood for her bluesy songs. But she was happy with her husband and the recording contract.

The big trouble was that her rewards had not come along in time to prevent her from experiencing the crushing pressures of her uncertain life as a woman and singer alone in show business. And she had grown up as a part-time waif and had lived in too lonely and naive a state of mind for too long, without anyone to educate her about the realities of the world.

If it seems that Billie had especially hard luck with her first husband and her boyfriends, it's also true that almost all of the women singers in those days had similar experiences. Men usually flocked around the successful singers and tried to take their money. Billie was no different from anyone else. But she had fewer defenses against the hustlers, because she had never been protected by men—or by anyone, really—from her earliest years. She had always eventually managed to get away from the people who were hurting and exploiting her. But she needed something to lean on and soothe her nerves and fears. Heroin had been her answer. She just kept taking it, although Louis tried to persuade her to stop again—and for good. Billie loved to get high.

Billie was terrified that the police were following her every move. Louis McKay later said that he believed her fears were unfounded in those days. She would have faced a very long prison term if she had been caught, and the police could easily have caught her. Nevertheless, she thought they were watching her, ready to pounce. To avoid airports, she made Louis drive her to most of her gigs, even if it meant that he had to drive for twenty hours at a time to get her from one gig to another clear across the country.

For years, Billie had wanted to sing in Europe. All of the other famous singers and instrumentalists whom she admired had performed there. Especially because she couldn't work in a club in New York, the dream of playing in Europe became very important to her. Leonard Feather, a jazz pianist, songwriter, and record producer who had made a name for himself most of all as a jazz critic, became the man in charge of Billie's first European tour, organized in 1954.

The show was called Jazz Club U.S.A. and starred Billie, whose accompanist then was Carl Drinkard. Vibes player Red Norvo and his trio, clarinetist Buddy De Franco and his quintet, and the fine pianist Beryl Booker and her women's trio also traveled for the tour.

Technical problems plagued it from the start, but Billie behaved like a trouper. She worked hard to find her stepmother, Fanny Holiday, who swore to Billie's identity, so that Billie could get a passport. The tour group was supposed to fly to Stockholm, Sweden, for the first concert. But such a heavy snow had fallen there that the plane couldn't land. It had to go on to Copenhagen, Denmark. Everyone got on a train bound for Sweden. The temperatures were bitter cold. Instruments were lost. Billie had trouble organizing a trio from the musicians booked on the tour. Some people were reluctant to play with her because of her reputation. She didn't always show up for performances, and when she did appear, she was not always in the best condition.

In Norvo's group, bassist Red Mitchell, who was making his first trip to Sweden with that tour, said he would be happy to play for her; so did a woman drummer named Elaine Leighton in Beryl Booker's trio. But the travel delay because of the weather meant there was no time for a rehearsal. All of the

Billie arrives in England in 1954.

groups had to perform without rest, a few hours after getting to Stockholm. Critics didn't like the performances by any of the groups.

Leonard Feather later reported that a hypodermic needle was found in Billie's dressing room the day after the show. But it may not have been hers. A Swedish musician who was known to be a junkie had come backstage to say hello after the performance. After that, there was no hint of trouble about Billie. "Her behavior was impeccable," Feather recalled in his book, *From Satchmo to Miles*.

Billie was thrilled to be in Europe. In Stockholm, she hired a taxi to take her for a tour around the city. Red Mitchell went along with her. Billie asked the driver to take them to the poor parts of the city. The driver told them that there weren't any sections like that. Both Billie and Red Mitchell were surprised and delighted to hear it. Red was so impressed that he eventually moved to Stockholm. Billie began to toy with the idea of spending a lot of time in Europe.

She caught a cold, which affected her voice. By the time the tour got to Copenhagen, she needed help. A doctor gave her medicine to soak in sugar and then swallow, she recalled. Leonard Feather was delighted to see how well Billie held up under the difficult conditions of the trip. She gave him no trouble at all. From Scandinavia, they went to Belgium, Germany, and France. Her recordings had preceded her by many years, and crowds turned out.

It didn't seem to matter to audiences that her voice had changed a little over the years. The staccato chirps were now more of a deliberate trick than a spontaneous, unexpected embellishment. Her nasal but musical whine, at one time both gay and melancholy within the same song, and even on the same note, had become more pronounced. Her voice sometimes made rather affected loop-the-loops, going up and down in curvy melody lines. Of course, she could hardly have failed to learn from experience what helped her communicate with audiences. They came to wrap themselves up in her eccentricities while she imitated her youthful style. But her mannerisms actually added to her charm. Her mature sound was so pleasing that audiences still loved her singing. Billie Holiday could explore music and do anything she liked for an audience. Her timing and her intonation were still wonderful. As a girl, her voice had glistened. Now it was dark and burnished. If at any time it wavered, that became part of her legend.

Feather watched the musicians work under hard conditions on the tour. Photographers jumped onstage while Billie was singing. In Cologne, Germany, one jumped up and exploded a flashgun within inches of her face while she was singing a poignant ending to "I Cover the Waterfront." The audience laughed and whistled, but Billie kept her poise. Whenever the musicians went to a club after a performance, Billie was usually asked to sing a song. No matter how tired she was, she obliged. Feather described her voice as "smooth and clear."

"I was not surprised by her cooperation and comportment throughout the tour," he wrote in *From Satchmo to Miles*. "Everything contrasted sharply with her life in America. Instead of the second-rate ghetto theaters, tacky dressing rooms, and half-empty, minor-league nightclubs in Detroit and Pittsburgh that typified her directionless career, she found . . . fans who had dreamed for years of seeing her, bouquets presented to her onstage and backstage, autograph hunters, deferential treatment—and never a glimpse of racism. When treated like a lady, she acted accordingly. Her morale was never better. . . . My most vivid memory of the tour is of her indomitable pride and firmness under pressure.

"One morning in Brussels, we missed the musicians' bus that was to take us to Frankfurt, West Germany. . . . We chased clear across Belgium in a taxi to the German border, then had to change there for a German cab all the way to Düsseldorf—and arrived shivering at the airport to find the last plane to Frankfurt had just left. A small plane was hastily chartered. It seated only four; since I was required to appear as the show's master of ceremonies, Louis McKay had to proceed by train. With the pilot . . . Billie and I huddled in the backseat and killed a small bottle of Steinhaegen, a remedy that did little to allay our incipient frostbite. We reached Frankfurt barely in time for the show. . . . Billie gave two magnificent performances that night, showing not a trace of the ordeal."

Two days later, Billie had a bad moment. "After a particularly grueling day's travel," Feather recounted, "she announced that she was calling Joe Glaser in New York to arrange for her immediate return home in midtour. Louis McKay assured us that she was just talking, and he was right." Feather also noticed that "McKay seemed to keep her in good mental and physical shape." At the end of the tour, Billie went on to appear at concerts on her own in England. One was given to a crowd of about six thousand at London's Albert Hall. That concert thrilled her as much as the one at Carnegie Hall had done when she had just gotten out of prison.

She said that Europe made her feel "truly alive." Leonard Feather thought that her whole life might have been different if she had enjoyed the kind of support as a budding teenage singer that she had found in Europe.

THE DRAMA CONTINUES

Reporters in England gathered in Billie's dressing room for a press conference. They were supposed to ask her about her career, but most of their questions centered on her legal troubles stemming from drugs. Billie was uncomfortable, but she tried to answer. "I'm trying to get my police card back," she said. Louis McKay, who was by her side, explained that she could earn another $75,000 a year if she could obtain a cabaret card again and perform in New York City clubs. "It's not just the dough, it's the principle of the thing. To me it's unfair," Billie said.

A British critic named Max Jones, who wrote for the country's leading jazz magazine, *Melody Maker*, rescued her from the questions about her personal drama. He asked her to reminisce about her musical influences and her friends among the musicians. Billie relaxed with his help. When Max Jones reviewed one of her performances, he wrote, "On stage she looks calm and dignified, but she also looks warm and sounds warm."

She was offered work in Europe and Africa, but she decided to head back to New York. Both Louis McKay and Joe Glaser wanted her there. News of her success in Europe had reached the States. The glamour she had acquired assured her of steady work at home. She was being offered very high fees to appear in concert and at clubs. If she could control her moodiness and her drug addiction, she could have the opportunity to make up to herself for all her lost time and her past troubles.

But she was living on an emotional roller coaster. She could endure breakdowns of cars and trains with strong spirit as she toured in England. Then a little incident—a thoughtless word, perhaps—could reduce her to tears. That's what happened backstage at Royal Albert Hall just after she had been treated to thunderous applause by the audience. Her unpredictable mood changes were hard for her, her husband, and her accompanists to cope with. But she loved to sing. She tried to keep going wherever her career led her. When she headed back to New York, her self-esteem and confidence had been bolstered by the respect she had earned in Europe.

One of her big triumphs after her homecoming took place at the very first concert of the Newport Jazz Festival in Rhode Island in July 1954. George Wein, who owned Storyville in Boston, made a priority of scheduling Billie to sing at his new festival. It was a star-studded affair. Some of Billie's old friends appeared with her. Pianist Teddy Wilson led the quintet, with Buck Clayton playing trumpet behind her. Tenor saxophonist Lester Young wasn't booked to play with her group, but he went onstage and joined it. They were friends again. Not long afterward, Teddy Wilson commented to a *Down Beat* writer that she had her "old magic."

She still couldn't convince the police in New York that they should give her a cabaret card. So she kept moving around the country, performing in clubs and concerts. *Down Beat* finally accorded her artistry the official tribute that she had hungered for since her days at Cafe Society Downtown. At an awards ceremony in California, the magazine gave her a trophy and called her "one of the all-time great vocalists in jazz." It had been sixteen years since Count Basie was quoted by *Melody Maker*: "Billie is a marvelous artist who remains unappreciated by the world at large."

Billie in a 1950s recording session

Despite her successes, Billie's mind kept wandering to the dark side of her experiences—the harassment, the scandals, the artistic slights, her long battle against heroin. She had also drunk too much alcohol and smoked too many cigarettes. She had never had a very wide vocal range—less than two octaves. Now her range was narrowing, and her voice was beginning to wear thin from the constant abuse. Her notes wavered at times. The plaintive, bluesy quality became more pronounced. When she sang "Gloomy Sunday," a song for which she was well known, the way she emphasized the word "gloomy" conjured up an image of dense gray clouds for as far as the eye could see. Nothing, however, dimmed the brightness and warmth of her vibrato and the sound of laughter in her swinging melody lines on a day when she was feeling fairly well.

She began to work with her friend Maely Dufty's husband, Bill, a journalist, on her life story, *Lady Sings the Blues*. She told him what she wanted him to know, and he tried to supply the rest and put the book in order. Lady's memory for dates wasn't very good. Sometimes it seemed that she toyed with the facts the way she did with formally written melody lines, improving them as she went along, but making it difficult for anyone to analyze them. And there were some things that she must have felt were too painful and embarrassing to pass on. Or else she may have forgotten the truth.

It was in the back of her mind that she wanted to return to Europe. But there were many opportunities for her to work in the United States and keep her name before the public, even if she couldn't sing in New York clubs. Her concerts in Europe became all the more tantalizing and popular for their rarity.

She went to work at the Showboat Club in Philadelphia. One morning in February 1956, the South Philadelphia hotel room that she and Louis shared was raided by the police. Billie was charged with possession of narcotics. The police also arrested Louis because they found an unlicensed pistol among his possessions. Billie was released on bail that afternoon so she could continue working at the club. Louis was held until the

*A troubled Billie leaves a Philadelphia jail
shortly after her 1956 arrest.*

evening, when he too was let go. He showed up in Billie's dressing room.

The police let them travel back to New York the next day. There they finally got married. And Billie decided it was time for her to try to break her habit again. She said that addicts could never be sure they were free of heroin until they were dead. She warned that the only thing heroin could do for people was kill them. She had every reason in the world to quit for her own good. Furthermore, Louis was always in legal jeopardy because he knew she was an addict. The police could view him with suspicion as an accomplice. She entered a clinic, where doctors weaned her away from heroin with the use of substitute drugs. They told her she could stay clean if she used her willpower and had a little good luck.

Billie sang lyrics about having been down so long that it didn't worry her to be that way. She could sound carelessly happy about that message. She had a gritty sense of humor. The increasing raspiness of her voice helped her interpret that song and the rest of her repertoire soulfully. But she had acquired the aura of an underdog in her sound as well as in her reputation. She began substituting alcohol for the heroin. Friends usually saw her with a glass of gin in her hand. She learned new songs, but she never sang them in performances. It was all she could do to keep track of the music and lyrics of the songs she had been singing for years.

When her book was published, her friends were surprised at how much the story differed from the facts they knew to be true. Bobby Tucker thought she had written the book to provide an entertaining story and make money. Critics, searching for grains of truth, tried to analyze her statements about herself. Only when she talked about music and musicians did she seem lucid, truthful, and informative.

No matter what facts Lady revealed, there was one underlying truth in her disorganized personal story: her life had been turbulent. She had scrambled to survive as a child. She had done everything she could to help feed and clothe herself, find a place in the sun, and steady her nerves, all the while coping with all kinds of parasites while she tried to succeed in the world.

She had common sense, but she had little education about the way the world worked. So she found herself fighting with everyone—club owners, musicians, boyfriends, and husbands—for various reasons. Early in life she was naive. Later on, drugs and alcohol confused her. She herself never wanted to cheat or belittle anyone else for the fun of it. The sweetness of her intentions was evident in her singing voice. But she had been neglected as a child. Though she rose to some heights in her career, she could also neglect herself and fall to abysmal lows.

Bobby Tucker thought that Billie might have really loved Jimmy Monroe, or even the married piano player she had met as a teenager, more than she cared for Louis McKay. Not everyone thought that Billie's marriage to Louis McKay was made in heaven. The couple fought a great deal. Fighting had become a habit for her. She enjoyed it and she didn't really know any other way to live. Musicians sometimes saw Billie and Louis out in the clubs, listening to music as members of the audience. Big Nick Nicholas, who played many instruments and sang in a rich baritone, often saw the couple at a club where he was performing regularly near Harlem. They seemed very happy together. Louis was attentive to Billie and protective of her.

But her moodiness didn't improve with her marriage to Louis. Her accompanist, Carl Drinkard, left her. She hired other accompanists who stayed with her only for short periods. Working with Billie could be stressful. Eventually, even Louis McKay made a tough decision about Billie. It signaled the beginning of the end for their marriage. He accepted a job as manager of a nightclub in Chicago. Billie sang there and then moved on to other engagements. Sometimes, but not always, McKay traveled with her. Many musicians avoided her because it was so difficult to spend time with her. Without warning, she got into fights with them.

She was drinking about two bottles of alcohol a day. She smoked constantly, too. Accompanists had to help her walk onto the stage. Musicians and fans who had idolized her for years sat in the audience and felt terrible to see what bad shape Billie had gotten herself into.

Pianist Mal Waldron, however, developed a great affection for Lady Day at this time. The first time he played for her, she was kind to him, acting like a big sister, advising him how to accompany her. When she offered him the job as her regular accompanist, he accepted instantly. He let her lean on him.

Billie moved into an apartment on West Eighty-seventh Street on Manhattan's Upper West Side, alone. There she drank too much at night while she smoked and watched television. By now Louis McKay was gone for good. He had moved to California. She was lonely without him, she told a friend. Her boxer, Mister, had died, but she had the company of another dog, a little Chihuahua. A girlfriend helped her with shopping, meals, and cleaning. A young musician ran errands for her. Otherwise, few people called or visited.

She kept pulling herself together to perform—at the Newport Jazz Festival, at the Shakespeare Festival in Ontario, Canada, and at broadcast and recording studios. Her recording contract with Verve had expired, and she hired a lawyer to help work out the royalty arrangement for a new contract with Columbia. The lawyer was surprised to discover how much Billie knew about contracts. Like most experienced artists, she really didn't need anyone's help in understanding a contract, but she wanted a lawyer to ask for advance money. She didn't like to bargain for herself.

In December 1957, she made the film for CBS-TV, *The Sound of Jazz*, which was included in the series, *The Seven Lively Arts*. Though her friends thought she looked thin and gaunt, she was still a stunning woman with her hair pulled straight back to emphasize her lovely face. There was a bright, dreamy, happy look in her eyes as she sang with Lester Young and her other friends. She had a magical stage presence.

She also kept her wits about her enough to know exactly what she wanted to do for her next recording. She wanted to perform with bandleader Ray Ellis and his orchestra, with strings. Columbia gave her everything she wanted. However, the contract included a provision that her lawyer had to make sure she got to the recording sessions on time.

Billie with her chihuahua

The sessions were scheduled for nighttime—the hours when she usually performed. She brought gin and Coca-Cola to the studio, and she drank several glasses of alcohol to get herself started. Unfortunately, it did not take much for her to get drunk by this time. The recording sessions stretched out for hours. Finally the record was done, with some wonderful musicians playing in the orchestra. The trombonists were particularly artful. Their sound suited Billie's voice perfectly. The violinists provided one of the most unexpected bonuses. All her life, people had talked about her "odd sound"—her high, feminine, whiny, musical, warm, and poignant soprano. When she was accompanied by violins, it became clear that the timbre of her voice had a strong kinship with the sound of those string instruments.

The album, which was called *Lady in Satin*, received mixed reviews. Some critics said it was pitiful. They were distressed at her raspy voice and wavering pitch. But her sound was soothing, too, and she had lost none of her ability to affect audiences with her rhythmic genius and musicality. Like a kitten with a ball of yarn, she could still play with lyrics—phrases, words, and even just syllables. She could push them around any way she liked and do cunning tricks with them. She thought *Lady in Satin* was the best album she had ever made. It was certainly one of the most controversial. Defying the critics, the legendary trumpeter Miles Davis, among other great experts, thought that Billie was communicating with the maturity of a great artist. He loved the album precisely because Billie's voice was in a state of ruin—but a majestic ruin.

A year later, in March 1959, Billie tried to follow it up with another album done with Ray Ellis. This time, though, her power to tell stories and convince an audience of her feelings was obviously gone. Her voice was too far out of control.

Undaunted, she wanted to keep performing. Carmen McRae, who idolized Billie as a role model for singing, said that Billie was happy only when she was singing. She celebrated her forty-fourth birthday in April by preparing a dinner party for her friends. They found her joking and cooking soul-

In performance in 1958

food—stuffed fish, beans, and such things. She laughed at Mal Waldron's jokes. He thought she had energy left. So far, she had foiled the doctors, who had been telling her for a while that she would have to quit drinking or she would die. Mal didn't see any sign of her taking drugs anymore, but off the bandstand she always had a glass of gin in her hand.

After her party she traveled to Boston to sing at Storyville owned by George Wein, a founder of the Newport Jazz Festival. From somewhere she found the strength to deliver "wonderful" performances for several weeks, Wein thought. So people thought it was possible that she could sing well for a concert scheduled at the Phoenix Theater in New York City on May 25, 1959. But she showed up looking totally worn out and far older than her age at the Phoenix. When Leonard Feather saw her backstage, his expression mirrored how upset he was about her appearance. "What's the matter, Leonard?" she said. "Seen a ghost or something?" She had to be helped onstage. She began by singing one of the songs she was famous for: "Ain't Nobody's Business If I Do." But she wasn't able to finish her second song. She left the stage and collapsed backstage.

Feather and others wanted to take her to a hospital, but Lady insisted on going home. Several weeks later a friend found her unconscious on the floor. She was rushed to Knickerbocker Hospital, where nobody recognized her name: Mrs. Eleanora McKay. She waited for an hour without treatment. Her personal doctor became involved, and she was transferred to Metropolitan Hospital, where she seemed to rally at times. But she was suffering from many ailments connected to her excesses, including cirrhosis of the liver caused by her drinking.

There was a bizarre twist to her story. The police had left her alone for the most part for years. But they arrested her in the hospital when someone found heroin in her room. Her doctor insisted that she couldn't have brought the heroin there herself. A visitor must have left it. Billie certainly didn't have the strength to take drugs. Nevertheless, the police fingerprinted her and

A huge crowd filled the sidewalks outside St. Paul the Apostle Church in New York for Billie Holiday's funeral on July 21, 1959.

took her photograph while she was lying flat on her back in bed, too weak to get up by herself. Some people say the police even handcuffed her to the bed. They stationed a guard at her door and took away the portable record player that had enabled her to listen to music and ease her distress.

When Louis McKay flew in from California, she told him, "Daddy, I didn't know they could be this cruel to nobody." It had been a terrible fight for her all the way. Louis went to see her every day. When she developed a kidney infection, she was put in an oxygen tent. The oxygen revived her enough so that she decided to sneak a cigarette. But the cigarette nearly caused a fire when it mixed with the oxygen.

She appeared not to realize that she was actually in danger of dying. She was working on plans for a film about her life, and she was hoping to be paid $100,000. She had already had an offer of $50,000. Bill Dufty brought her an advance of $750 and taped the cash to her leg. It was for a series of articles that he would write with her about her life. She had nothing else to her name that day.

Her body was giving up. Just before dawn on July 17, a Sunday, Billie Holiday died of congestive heart failure. In Greenwich Village, some musicians put Billie's recording of "Gloomy Sunday," one of her most mournful-sounding songs, on a record player and played it over and over again. Thousands of people went to the funeral service on July 21 at Saint Paul the Apostle Church in New York. Important and powerful critics, musicians, concert and record producers, and club owners showed up, as did many fans. The funeral procession made a detour to let Billie's body pass through Harlem one last time. Mal Waldron recalled that she had joked with him about how she didn't want to be buried. She wanted to be cremated and have her ashes tossed from a plane. But she was buried next to her mother in Saint Raymond's Cemetery in the Bronx.

As her only heir, Louis McKay would soon have a windfall. There was a sudden surge of interest in Billie's recordings. Royalties from the sales reportedly soon amounted to about $100,000. Louis McKay eventually put a marker on her grave, though not right away. Then a legion of protégés talked about her to their audiences and sang her songs. Their memories and praise helped to keep her legacy alive.

Her recordings never lost their appeal and were played often on the radio. Her life story, which had fascinated filmmakers for so long, was made into a film in 1971. Called *Lady Sings the Blues*, with a fine dramatic performance by singer Diana Ross, it was released in 1972. The filmmakers changed many of the facts of Billie's life even more than she had done in her book. Her recordings weren't used for the sound track. Ross, a popular singer, sang Billie's tunes, but she had a totally different sound and style from Billie's.

The film showed Lady Day in the throes of trying to kick drug addiction in a jail cell. There were also funny and touching scenes with her husband, Louis McKay. And the majority of moviegoers, who knew far less about Billie than they did about such jazz singers as the healthy, well-organized and cheerful-sounding Ella Fitzgerald, or the pretty, ambitious Motown star Diana Ross, became curious about Billie. They started to buy her records in large quantities.

Like Charlie Parker, the alto saxophonist who had invented the modern jazz style called bebop and who had died young from complications caused by drug addiction, Billie ceased to be a shadowy, mysterious memory once the film came out and her recordings were reissued. Her life was romanticized. She began to be elevated to the status of a legend.

All of the facts of her existence before she went from Baltimore to Harlem and became a powerful influence on jazz everywhere in the world may never be known. But in her artistry she conquered all of her problems. The triumph of her sound and style and unique, immediately recognizable voice has outshone the tawdriness of her troubles. Her recordings are still being reissued and played on the radio and in many public places—especially in Paris, London, and New York. They are used on the sound tracks of films. Young singers and musicians keep recording her songs and naming their albums *A Tribute to*

Billie Holiday. Some of them write songs based on the chords in the songs that she wrote. Of all the jazz singers who died long ago, only Bing Crosby, Louis Armstrong, Nat "King" Cole, and Lady have their music played all the time. And each time, Lady is reanimated.

SELECTED BIBLIOGRAPHY

Countless articles have appeared in magazines and newspapers such as the *New Yorker*, *Down Beat*, *Melody Maker* in London, *Time*, *Newsweek*, *The New York Times*, the *Los Angeles Times*, the *New York Post*, and *New York Daily News*. These articles have served both as general and specific background for this book. Where directly quoted, the periodicals are mentioned in the body of the book.

The following books served as primary sources:

Chilton, John. *Billie's Blues*. New York: Stein and Day, 1975.

Clarke, Donald. *Wishing on the Moon*. New York: Viking/Penguin Books USA Inc., 1994.

Clayton, Buck. *Buck Clayton's Jazz World*. New York: Oxford University Press, 1987.

Clooney, Rosemary, with Raymond Strait. *This for Remembrance*. Chicago: Playboy Press, 1977.

Feather, Leonard. *From Satchmo to Miles*. Briarcliffe Manor,

NY: Stein and Day, 1974.

Forrest, Helen, with Bill Libby. *I Had the Craziest Dream*. New York: Coward, McCann & Geoghegan, 1981.

Gourse, Leslie. *Louis' Children*. New York: William Morrow, 1984.

Holiday, Billie, with William Dufty. *Lady Sings the Blues*. New York: Doubleday and Co., 1956.

Kliment, Bud. *Billie Holiday*. New York: Chelsea House Publishers, 1990.

O'Meally, Robert. *Lady Day: The Many Faces of Billie Holiday*. New York: Arcade Publishing, 1991.

SELECTED DISCOGRAPHY

Billie's recordings have been reissued many times since her death. Some of those reissues, and even recordings issued before she died, can occasionally be found in secondhand record stores such as Footlights Records on 113 East Twelfth Street between Fourth and Third avenues in Greenwich Village, New York City.

Notable, out-of-print collections have been:

Billie Holiday: The Golden Years; a boxed collection of LPs of her Columbia recordings from 1933 through 1941. This collection shows Billie Holiday at the start of her career, when her voice was fresh and clear.

Billie Holiday, 1946–1959 on Verve; a collection of ten LPs that showcases Billie in her middle and late years.

Selections included in these two collections have been reissued as single LPs, cassettes, and CDs, many of which are currently available in record stores selling newly released albums.

Easier to find in secondhand record stores and less expensive than a boxed collection is:

Lady in Satin, Billie Holiday with Ray Ellis and His Orchestra, issued as a single LP, recorded in February 1958, for Columbia. This is the controversial album showing the deteriorated but affecting voice of Billie Holiday toward the end of her career. The album is included in the large Verve collection mentioned above.

The following titles are available in stores selling currently issued albums:

16 Most Requested Songs, on Legacy Records, in CD and cassette with "Body and Soul," "Gloomy Sunday," "I'm a Fool to Want You," "Why Was I Born?," "Easy Living," "My Man," "I'm Gonna Lock My Heart and Throw Away the Key," "Miss Brown to You," "If You Were There," "These Foolish Things," "The Way You Look Tonight," "Pennies from Heaven," "I Can't Give You Anything but Love," "I've Got My Love to Keep Me Warm," and "Carelessly."

Billie Holiday, 1933–1937, on the Classics label, CD only, with "Your Mother's Son-in-Law" (her first recording), "Did I Remember?," "Summertime," "Billie's Blues," "They Can't Take That Away from Me," "Me Myself and I," "One Two Button Your Shoe," "I've Got My Love to Keep Me Warm," "If My Heart Could Only Talk," "Let's Call the Whole Thing Off," "Born to Love," and "Without Your Love."

Billie Holiday and Her Orchestra, (1937–1939), on the Classics label, CD only, with "I Can't Get Started," "That's All I Ask of You," "Trav'lin' All Alone," "He's Funny That Way," "I Can't Get Started," "If I Were You," "Back in Your Own Backyard," and others.

Billie Holiday at Monterey, 1958, on the Black Hawk label, CD only, with "Ain't Nobody's Business If I Do," "Willow Weep for Me," "When Your Lover Has Gone," "God Bless the Child," "I Only Have Eyes for You," "Good Morning Heartache," "Them There Eyes," "Billie's Blues," "What a Little Moonlight Can Do," "Trav'lin' Light," and "Lover Come Back to Me."

Billie Holiday at Storyville, 1953, on the Black Lion label, CD only, originally released in 1953, with "Willow Weep for Me," "I Cover the Waterfront," "Too Marvelous for Words," "Ain't Nobody's Business If I Do," "Billie's Blues," "Them There Eyes," "Lover Come Back to Me," "Miss Brown to You," "He's Funny That Way," "You Go to My Head," "I Only Have Eyes For You," and "I Loves You, Porgy."

Billie Holiday, on the Bella Musica label, CD and cassette, with "Strange Fruit," "Lady Sings the Blues," "God Bless the Child," "A Fine Romance," "But Not for Me," "Stars Fell on Alabama," "I Wished on the Moon," "Sophisticated Lady," "I Cried for You," "Cheek to Cheek," "Let's Call the Whole Thing Off," "Our Love Is Here to Stay," "Too Marvelous for Words," "April in Paris," "Moonlight in Vermont," "Love Me or Leave Me," "Speak Low," and "Willow Weep for Me."

Billie's Best, on Verve, CD and cassette, with "What a Little Moonlight Can Do," "Some Other Spring," "All the Way," "Come Rain or Come Shine," "Comes Love," "He's Funny That Way," "Stars Fell on Alabama," "Gone with the Wind," "They Can't Take That Away from Me," "East of the Sun," "Everything I Have Is Yours," "Stormy Blues," "Speak Low," "April in Paris," and "I've Got My Love to Keep Me Warm."

Billie's Blues, on the Blue Note label, CD and cassette, with "Billie's Blues," "My Man," "What a Little Moonlight Can Do," "Trav'lin' Light," "I Cover the Waterfront," "All of Me," "Blue Turning Gray over You," "I Cried for You," "Detour Ahead," "Rocky Mountain Blues," "Them There Eyes," "Blue Moon," "Be Fair to Me."

Body and Soul, on the Verve label, cassette only, with "Body and Soul," "They Can't Take That Away from Me," "Darn That Dream," "Comes Love," "Gee, Baby, Ain't I Good to You," "Embraceable You," "Moonlight in Vermont," and "Let's Call the Whole Thing Off."

Classic Live Recordings, on JCI Associated Labels, CD only.

The Complete Billie Holiday on Verve, issued by Polygram, is a 10-CD box set. This is a reissue of the above-mentioned box collection of LPs available at secondhand and out-of-print record stores. The CD collection won three Grammys for 1993 for liner notes by such people as Buck Clayton and Phil Schaap, for packaging, and for overall quality. An excellent discography of all Billie Holiday's recorded works was included in the LP collection, *Billie Holiday on Verve, 1946–1959,* prepared by Akira Yamato, 1985.

INDEX

127

ABOUT THE AUTHOR

Leslie Gourse has done research and has written stories for major news organizations, including CBS and *The New York Times*. Since 1974, Ms. Gourse has been a freelance writer for many major magazines and newspapers covering general culture, social trends, and music. Her most recent books have been about current and historic New York City, jazz musicians, and jazz history. She lives in New York City.